Excel 2019
Basics

A Quick and Easy Guide to Boosting Your Productivity with Excel

NATHAN GEORGE

CONTENTS

Introduction...9

Who Is This Book For?...9

How to Use This Book..10

Assumptions...10

Practice Files..11

Improvements in Excel 2019..............................12

1. Getting Started with Excel.............................13

1.1 Creating a New Excel Workbook....................15

Create A Workbook Based on A Template...........15

Saving Your Excel Workbook.............................17

Open an Existing Workbook...............................18

Close a Workbook..19

1.2 The Excel User Interface................................20

1.3 Using AutoSave...23

Restoring a Previous Version.............................23

Renaming Your Workbook..................................24

Switching off AutoSave......................................25

1.4 Customising the Ribbon................................26

1.5 Getting Help in Excel....................................29

Tell Me Help Feature...29

2. Entering and Editing Data.............................31

2.1 Entering and Editing Data Manually..............31

2.2 Using AutoFill...32

2.3 Using Flash Fill..36

3. Design and Organise Workbooks...................39

3.1 Adding New Worksheets................................39

Naming a Worksheet...40

3.2 Moving and Copying Worksheets..................41

Removing a Worksheet..42

Hide a Worksheet 42

3.3 Freezing Rows and Columns..43

3.4 Applying Themes to Your Worksheet 45

Removing a Theme...45

4. Organising Your Data.. 46

4.1 Copying, Moving and Deleting Data............................46

Selecting a Group of Cells 46

Deselecting Cells 47

Copying and Pasting Data 47

Moving Data..48

Insert or Delete Rows and Columns 49

4.2 Find and Replace Data 51

4.3 Sorting Data...53

Quick Sort...53

Custom Sort...54

Sorting with a Custom List..55

4.4 Filtering Data 57

Applying a Custom Filter...58

Changing the Sort Order of a Filtered List.......................61

Removing a Filter...61

5. Formatting Cells.. 62

5.1 Arrange Cells, Rows and Columns 62

Resizing Rows and Columns..62

Resizing Cells with the Cells Format Command 63

Hide Rows and Columns 65

Hide and Unhide a Worksheet 65

Applying Cell Styles...66

Merging Cells and Aligning Data.....................................66

5.2 Applying Number Formats..69

5.3 Copy Cell Formatting 74

5.4 Conditional Formatting..76

    Use Multiple Conditional Formats...77

    Formatting Text Fields..77

    Conditionally Formatting Time 78

    Creating Conditional Formatting Rules.......................................79

6. Carrying out Calculations with Formulas.........................83

6.1 Operators in Excel 84

    Arithmetic Operators 84

    Comparison Operators 84

    Operator Precedence..85

    Parentheses and Operator Precedence 85

6.2 Entering a Formula 86

6.3 Calculating Percentages 88

6.4 The AutoSum Tool 90

    Using AutoSum with Non-contiguous data 92

    Using AutoSum with Different Ranges...93

    Using AutoSum for Other Aggregate Functions...........................94

6.5 Quick Sum with the Status Bar 96

6.6 Calculating Date and Time...97

    Adding Time...97

    Subtracting Time..99

    Calculating Time Across Days..100

    Using the TIME function...100

    Adding and Subtracting Dates 101

6.7 Relative and Absolute Cell Reference 103

    Relative Cell Reference 103

    Absolute Cell Reference..103

    Mixed Cell Reference 106

6.8 Using Data from Other Worksheets 107

7. Creating Data Validation Rules......................................109

    How to Add a Data Validation Rule...110

How to Edit or Remove Data Validation Rules 113

8. Named Ranges..114

8.1 Creating a Named Range...116

8.2 Editing a Named Range...117

8.3 Deleting a Named Range 118

8.4 How to Use a Named Range 118

9. Working with Functions 120

9.1 How to Enter a Function...121

Using the Insert Function Dialogue Box 122

9.2 Aggregate Functions 126

SUM Function 126

AVERAGE Function...129

MAX, MIN, MEDIAN Functions..................................131

COUNT Function 132

9.3 Conditional Functions 135

IF Function 135

Nested IF Functions...139

Advanced IF Functions 140

9.4 Date Functions...144

DATE Function..144

DATEDIF Function 149

DAYS Function 151

9.5 Find Data with VLOOKUP...153

9.6 Manipulate Text..155

LEN Function 155

MID Function 156

9.7 Accessing More Functions in Excel 159

Getting More Help with Functions 160

10. Working with Tables 161

10.1 Create an Excel Table..163

10.2 Choosing a Table Style 165

How to Apply a Table Style 165

Configure Table Style Options 166

10.3 Sorting Data in a Table 167

Sort by One Column 167

Sort by Multiple Columns 167

10.4 Filtering Table Data 169

Applying a Custom Filter 170

10.5 Adding a Totals Row to Your Table 172

10.6 Removing Table Attributes 173

11. Introduction to Pivot Tables 174

11.1 Preparing Your Data 174

11.2 Creating a Pivot Table 176

Summarising Data by Date 181

Applying Formatting 183

11.3 Filter and Sort a PivotTable 184

Applying a Custom Filter 185

Sorting PivotTable Data 185

12. Creating Charts 186

12.1 Creating a Chart via the Quick Analysis Tool 188

12.2 Creating a Chart via the Excel Ribbon 190

12.3 Customising Charts 192

Switching the X and Y Axes 193

Change the Data Source 194

Adding Axis Titles 196

Chart Styles 198

12.4 Creating Sparkline Charts 200

Formatting a Sparkline Chart 201

13. Printing Your Worksheet 202

Page Setup 202

Setting the Print Area 204

Preview and Print Your Worksheet 205

14. Securing Your Workbook 208

How to set a password for your Excel workbook....................................208

Removing a Password from an Excel File..210

Afterword: Next Steps...**211**

Appendix: Keyboard Shortcuts (Excel for Windows).......................**212**

Access Keys for Ribbon Tabs..214

Glossary...**215**

Index **218**

About the Author **220**

Other Books by Author...**221**

INTRODUCTION

Excel 2019 Basics covers all you would need to successfully create workbooks with Excel to provide solutions for your data. Starting from the basics, you learn how to create, edit, format, and print your worksheets. You learn how to carry out different types of calculations with formulas and functions, how to work with Excel tables, how to summarize data from different perspectives with pivot tables, and how to present your data with different types of charts.

This book is concise and to the point as you don't need to wade through a wall of text to learn how to quickly carry out a task in Excel. Hence you will not see the unnecessary verbosity and filler text you may find in some other Excel books in this book. The aim is to take even a complete beginner to someone that is skilled in Excel within a few short hours.

Who Is This Book For?

Excel 2019 Basics starts from the basics so is suitable for you if you're new to Excel or spreadsheets in general. This book is also for you if you have some Excel skills and you're looking to expand on that by learning the new features in Excel 2019.

The necessary topics have been covered to give you a solid foundation and the tools to create solutions for your data. However, the topics have been kept at a level to not be overwhelming to someone completely new to Excel and interested in a quick course without getting bogged down with the more advanced topics.

If you need something more advanced, like What-If Analysis, macros, advanced functions, in-depth pivot tables etc. then this book is not for you. It might be a good idea to examine the table of contents first to see if it covers your requirements.

This book is aimed at readers with Microsoft Excel 2019, however, many of the core Excel features remain the same for earlier versions of the software like Excel 2016, 2013, and 2010. So, you would still find many of the lessons in this book relevant even if you have an earlier version of Excel.

As much as possible, I point out the features new in Excel 2019 when covered. Note however that if you're using an earlier version of Excel, some of the file related tasks described in this book may not match your old version of Excel. This is due to Microsoft changing command options and the screens for many file-related tasks compared to older versions.

How to Use This Book

This book can be used as a step-by-step training guide as well as a reference manual that you come back to from time to time. You can read it cover to cover or skip to certain parts that cover topics you want to learn. Although the chapters have been organised in a logical manner, the book has been designed to enable you to read a chapter as a standalone tutorial to learn how to carry out a certain task.

There are many ways to carry out the same task in Excel, so, for brevity, I have focused on the most efficient way of carrying out a task. On some occasions, however, I also provided alternative ways to carry out a task.

As much as possible, the menu items and commands mentioned are bolded to distinguish them from the other text. I have also included many images to illustrate the features and tasks being discussed.

Assumptions

The software and hardware assumptions made when writing this book is that you already have Excel 2019 installed on your computer and that you're working on the Windows 10 platform.

Important: Excel 2019 is the first version of Excel that is not compatible with previous versions of Windows. If you have an earlier version of Windows, for example, Windows 7 or 8, and you're subscribed to Office 365, then the newest version of Excel you can run will be Excel 2016.

Excel 2016 has all the power of Excel 2019 apart from a few added features and some screens that look different. If you are running Excel 2016 you can still use this book (as long as you're aware that some of the screens shown may look slightly different). Alternatively, you can get my *Excel 2016 Basics* book which is the previous version of this book.

If you are using Excel 2019 on a Mac, then simply substitute any Windows keyboard commands mentioned in the book for the Mac equivalent. All the features within Excel remain the same for both platforms.

If you're using Excel on a tablet or touchscreen device, again, simply substitute any keyboard commands mentioned in the book with the equivalent on your touchscreen device.

Practice Files

Downloadable .xlsx files have been provided to enable you to follow some examples in this book without needing to create the data from scratch. You can practice by changing the data to view different results. Please note that practice files have been included only for examples using a sizable amount of data. You can click on the following link to download the file.

https://s3.amazonaws.com/ngdigital/Excel2019BasicsPracticeFiles.zip

Note: You would need to have Excel installed on your computer to open and use these files (preferably Excel 2010 and above). Also, the files have been zipped into one download. Windows 10 comes with the functionality to unzip files but if your OS does not have this functionality, you'll need to get a piece of software like WinZip or WinRAR to unzip the file.

Improvements in Excel 2019

Ink Improvements

Improved inking and drawing features are available under Draw that enable you to use a drawing tablet to enter math formulas or freestyle drawing in your worksheet.

Better Cell Selection

Have your ever selected too many cells on your worksheet or the wrong ones? You can now deselect cells you don't want to be part of your selection without having to start over.

Improved Autocomplete

The autocomplete is 'smarter' in Excel 2019. For example, let's say you want to use the FORMULATEXT function, but you can't remember the exact spelling, you can just type in =TEXT and the autocomplete menu will list all the functions that contain "TEXT" in their name, including FORMULATEXT. In previous editions, you would need to start spelling the name correctly for autocomplete to find it.

Office Themes

You can now apply three Office Themes to Excel: Colorful, Dark Gray, Black, and White. To change your Excel theme, go to **File > Account** and then select a theme from the **Office Theme** drop-down list. Note that the theme you choose will be applied across all your Office 365 applications.

Translate Words to Other Languages

You can now translate a word or phrase to another language with Microsoft Translator. You can access this feature from the **Translate** button on the **Review** tab in the ribbon.

1. GETTING STARTED WITH EXCEL

C lick on the Windows start menu and scroll down to the group of applications starting with E. You'll see Excel as part of the list.

To be able to access Excel faster next time you can pin it to the **Start menu**, **Taskbar**, or place a shortcut on your **desktop**.

To pin Excel to your Start menu:

1. Click on the Windows **Start menu**.

2. Scroll down to the group of applications under **E**.

3. Right-click **Excel** and select **Pin to Start**.

To pin Excel to your Taskbar:

1. Click on the **Start menu**.

2. Scroll down to the group of applications under **E**.

3. Right-click **Excel** and select **More** > **Pin to taskbar**.

To place a copy of Excel's shortcut on your desktop:

1. Click on the **Start menu**.

2. Right-click on **Excel** and select **More > Open file location**. This will open the shortcut folder location of Excel.

3. In the folder, right-click on Excel and click on **Copy**.

4. On your desktop, right-click any area and select **Paste**.

1.1 Creating a New Excel Workbook

Launch Excel from the start menu or the icon you have created on your taskbar or desktop.

Excel will launch to the **Home** screen. The Excel 2019 start screen enables you to create a new blank workbook or open one of your recently opened workbooks. You also have a selection of predefined templates that you can use as the basis of your workbook.

To create a new workbook, click on **Blank workbook**. This will create a new workbook with a worksheet named **Sheet1**.

Tip: Another way to quickly create a new workbook when you already have a workbook open is to press **CTRL + N** on your keyboard. This will create a new workbook.

Create A Workbook Based on A Template

To create a new workbook based on one of Excel's predefined templates, click on the **New** button on the left navigation pane to go to the New screen. The categories of available templates are listed on the top of the screen next to **Suggested searches**.

You can narrow down the displayed templates by clicking on one of the categories - Business, Personal, Planners and Trackers, Lists, Budgets, Charts or Calendars.

Once you identify the template you'll like to use, double click on it to create a new worksheet based on it.

Saving Your Excel Workbook

To save your workbook for the first time:

1. Click the disk icon on Quick Access Toolbar (the top-left of the window) or click on the **File** tab and this will open the Backstage view.

2. Click **Save As** (you'll see **Save a Copy** if your file has been previously saved to OneDrive).

3. On the next screen, click on **OneDrive – Personal** (if you're using OneDrive) or **This PC** (if you're not saving it to OneDrive).

4. On the right side of the page, you get a text box to enter the file name. Enter the name of your worksheet here.

5. If you want to save it to a folder/sub-folder, navigate to the folder by double-clicking on the folder.

6. Click on the **Save** button to save the workbook.

You'll be taken back to the **Home** tab after the file has been saved.

Note: If your workbook has been previously saved to OneDrive or SharePoint and **AutoSave** is set to on, you'll have **Save a Copy** in place of **Save As**. You can use Save a Copy to save your workbook as a different file.

When you save a file, you overwrite the previous version of the file. If you want to keep an old version of the file while continuing to work on it, then you need to use **Save As** (or **Save a Copy**) as described above. This would save the workbook you're working on as a new file while the old version remains unchanged.

Tip: For a quicker way to save your workbook, after the first save, you can use the **Ctrl + S** shortcut keys. For a list of the most frequently used shortcuts in Excel 2019, see the Appendix.

Open an Existing Workbook

Click on **File** to display the Backstage view, and then click **Open** or press **Ctrl+O**.

On the **Open** page of the Backstage view you'll see the following options:

- **Recent**: To open a recent workbook, select **Recent** and click on the workbook you want to open on the right.

- **OneDrive - Personal**: To open a workbook from OneDrive, click on OneDrive - Personal and select your file from the right.

  Note: If you're not in the root folder of OneDrive you can use the blue up-arrow to navigate to the folder that contains your workbook.

- **This PC**: To open a workbook from the Documents local folder on your PC, click on **This PC** to display the Documents folder. Navigate to the folder containing your workbook. Click on the file to open it.

- **Browse**: To browse for a file on your computer, click the **Browse** button, and then use the Open dialogue box to find the file you want to open, select the file, and click on the **Open** button.

Close a Workbook

Ensure you've saved the workbook (if you want to keep the changes).

Click on **File** to display the Backstage view, and then click **Close**.

Or

Press the **Ctrl+W** shortcut keys to close the workbook.

1.2 The Excel User Interface

This section provides an overview of the Excel 2019 user interface so that you're familiar with the names for various parts of the interface that will be mentioned throughout the book.

The **Ribbon** contains the bulk of the commands in Excel arranged into a series of tabs from Home to Help.

The **File** button/tab opens the Backstage view when clicked. The Backstage view has several menu options including Home, New, Open, Info, Save, Save As, Print, Share, Export, Publish, and Close. At the bottom of the list, you have the Account menu option where you view your user information. You also have Options where you can change many of Excel's default settings.

Note that if your Excel workbook is saved on OneDrive, and you have AutoSave set to On, you'll not see the **Save As** menu option, instead, you'll have **Save a Copy** in its place.

To exit the Backstage view, click on the back button (the left-pointing arrow at the top-left of the page).

The **Quick Access Toolbar** is an area where you can add commands that you can quickly access, hence the name. To add a command to the quick access bar, click on the drop-down arrow to get a pop-up list, then check the command you want to add.

The **Home** tab provides the most used set of commands. The other tabs provide command buttons for specific tasks like inserting objects into your spreadsheet, formatting the page layout, working with formulas, working with datasets, reviewing your spreadsheet etc.

The **Worksheet area** contains the cells that will hold your data. The row headings are numbered while the column headings have letters. Each cell is identified by the combination of the column letter and row number. So, for example, the first cell on the sheet is A1, the second cell in the first row is B1 and the second cell in the first column is A2. You use these references to identify the cells on the worksheet.

A **workbook** is the Excel document itself. A **worksheet** is a sheet inside a workbook. Each workbook can have several worksheets. You can use the tabs at the bottom of the screen to name, move, copy, and delete worksheets. The plus (+) button next to the name tab enables you to add a new worksheet.

The **Formula bar** displays the contents of the active cell including any formula.

The **Status bar** provides information on the current display mode and allows you to zoom in and out of your spreadsheet by clicking on the plus (+) and minus (-) signs at the bottom-right of the screen.

The **Dialog Box Launcher** is a diagonal arrow in the lower-right corner of some groups. When clicked, it opens a dialogue box containing additional command options related to that group. So, if you cannot see a command on the Ribbon for a task you want to carry out, click on the small dialog box launcher to display more options for that group.

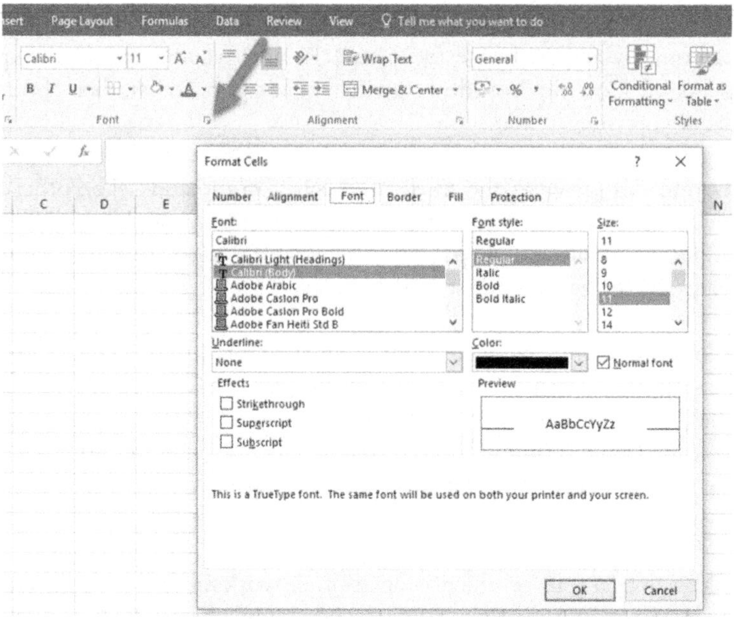

Page Layout
Formulas
Data
Review
View
Tell me what you want to do
Calibri
11
Wrap Text
Merge & Center
General
Conditional Formatting
Format as Table
Font
Alignment
Number
Styles
Format Cells
Number
Alignment
Font
Border
Fill
Protection
Font:
Calibri
Calibri Light (Headings)
Calibri (Body)
Adobe Arabic
Adobe Caslon Pro
Adobe Caslon Pro Bold
Adobe Fan Heiti Std B
Font style:
Regular
Regular
Italic
Bold
Bold Italic
Size:
11
8
9
10
11
12
14
Underline:
None
Color:
Normal font
Effects
Strikethrough
Superscript
Subscript
Preview
AaBbCcYyZz
This is a TrueType font. The same font will be used on both your printer and your screen.
OK
Cancel

1.3 Using AutoSave

AutoSave is a feature in the Quick Access Toolbar that is enabled when a file is stored on OneDrive or SharePoint. It automatically saves your changes every few seconds as you are working. The main advantage of AutoSave is that if your PC were to crash for any reason, your changes right up to the point it crashed would have been saved to disk, hence you'll hardly lose any work.

With AutoSave on, the **Save As** menu option in the backstage view is replaced by **Save a Copy**. If you normally use **File** > **Save As** after amending your workbook, it is recommended that you use **File** > **Save a Copy** before making your changes. That way, AutoSave will not overwrite the original file with the changes but the copy.

If like me, you're in the habit of just closing the workbook without saving, if you do not want to keep the changes, then AutoSave becomes an issue. In that case, you can turn off AutoSave before you make any changes and then save your workbook manually if you want to keep the changes.

While **AutoSave** is on if you make a mistake that you want to undo, ensure you use the **Undo** button (on the Quick Access Toolbar) to undo the changes before closing the workbook.

Restoring a Previous Version

You can also restore a previous version of your workbook from the Version History.

To restore an older version from the Version History list, do the following:

1. At the top of the window, click the file name.

2. Click on **Version History**.

   A **Version History** pane is displayed on the right of the screen that shows you the different versions of your document and the time they were saved. The versions are grouped under the day the file was saved. Look at the dates and times to find the version that you want to restore.

3. Double click the version that you want to restore, and this will open the workbook in a second window.

4. To revert to this version, click the **Restore** button that is displayed just under the ribbon.

Renaming Your Workbook

You can rename a previously saved workbook from the popup screen that is displayed when you click the file name at the top of the screen. In the **Name** field, you can enter a name for the workbook and press enter to rename the workbook.

Switching off AutoSave

Switching off AutoSave is not recommended. However, if you want to be able to just close Excel and discard all changes, whenever you wish, then you could turn off AutoSave for that particular file and manually save your workbook.

The default setting for AutoSave is **On** for files that are on the cloud (OneDrive or SharePoint). However, if you turn AutoSave **Off** for a particular workbook, Excel will remember the setting and will keep it off every time you reopen that workbook. If you switch it back to On, it will remember to keep it on for that workbook.

1.4 Customising the Ribbon

The area of the screen containing the tabs and command buttons is called the **ribbon**. You can customise the ribbon to your liking by adding or removing tabs and command buttons.

To customise the ribbon, right-click anywhere on the ribbon, below the tabs, and select **Customize the Ribbon...** from the pop-up menu.

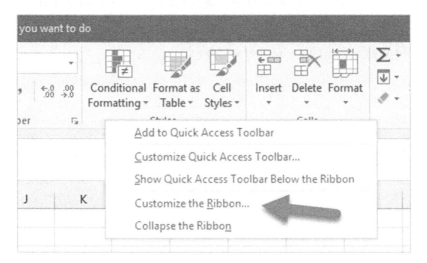

This will open the **Excel Options** window.

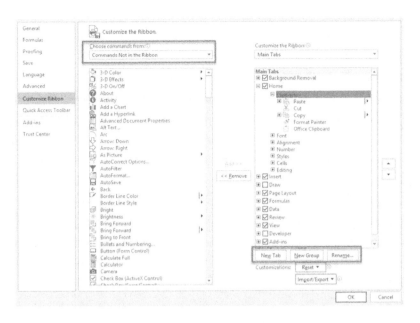

In the **Excel Options** window, the **Customize Ribbon** page will be selected, and on that page, you have two main boxes. On the right, you have the box that shows your current tabs - **Main Tabs**. On the left, you have the command buttons that you can add to the ribbon.

To expand a group in the **Main Tabs** box, click on the plus sign (+) to the left of an item. To collapse a group, click on the minus sign (-).

To find commands that are not currently on your ribbon, click the down arrow on the left box (named **Choose commands from)** and select **Commands Not in the Ribbon** from the drop-down list.

You will see a list of commands that are not on your ribbon. This is useful as it filters out the commands that are already on your ribbon.

Note: You cannot add or remove the default commands on the ribbon, but you can uncheck them on the list to prevent them from being displayed. Also, you cannot add command buttons to the default groups. You must create a new group to add a new command button.

To create a new tab:

Click on the **New Tab** button to create a new tab. Within the tab, you must create at least one group before you can add a command button from the left side of the screen.

To create a custom group:

Select the tab in which you want to create the group. This could be one of the default tabs or the new one you've created. Click on the **New Group** button (located at the bottom of the screen, under the Main Tabs box). This will create a new group within the currently selected tab. Select the new group and click on **Rename** to give the group your preferred name. You now have a custom group in which you can add commands.

To add commands to your custom group:

1. Select your custom group in the list on the right side of the screen.

2. Select the new command button you want to add from the list on the left side of the screen.

3. Click on the **Add >>** button to add the command to the new custom group.

4. If you want to remove a command from your custom group, select the command on the right box and click **<< Remove**.

5. Click **OK** to confirm the change.

When you view the customised tab on the ribbon, you'll see your new group and the command buttons you've added.

1.5 Getting Help in Excel

To access help in Excel, click on the **Help** command button on the Help tab on the ribbon. This will display the Help pane on the right side of the screen. You can use this pane to search for the topic you want help on.

A quick way to access help is to press the **F1** key on your keyboard (while Excel is the active window). This will display the Help pane on the right side of the screen.

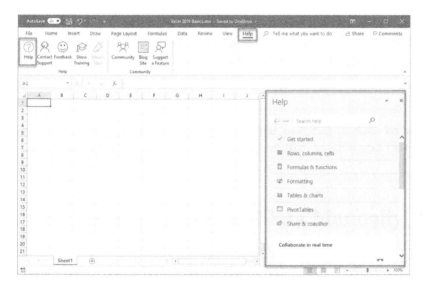

Tell Me Help Feature

Another way to get help in Excel is to use the **Tell Me** help feature (Alt+Q). This is a fairly new Office 365 feature which was introduced in Excel 2016. Tell Me provides a text field on the ribbon called **Tell me what you want to do** where you can enter words or phrases regarding actions you want to perform or a topic for which you want help.

Depending on the topic or how direct your question is, Tell Me will either list the steps needed to complete the task, take you to the appropriate screen, or display helpful information related to the topic in the Help pane.

When you click on **Tell me what you want to do,** a search box is displayed. Enter a search term to display a drop-down list of options related to your

move the cell pointer from cell to cell. To use the arrow keys when editing data, select the cell then click in the formula bar to edit the data there.

To overwrite data, click in the cell to make it the active cell and just type in the new value. This will overwrite the previous value.

If you only want to edit parts of the data in a cell, for example, a piece of text, then select the cell and click in the formula bar to edit the contents there.

Deleting data:

To delete data from your worksheet, select the data and hit the **Delete** key.

Default content alignment:

In Excel, numbers and formulas are right-aligned in the cell by default. Everything else is left-aligned by default. So, you can tell if Excel recognises your entry as a number or text value.

2.2 Using AutoFill

The Autofill feature in Excel enables you to fill cells with a series of sequential dates and numbers. It enables you to automate repetitive tasks as it is smart enough to figure out what data goes in a cell, based on another cell, when you drag the fill handle across cells.

Entering Dates with AutoFill

You may have a worksheet where you need to enter dates. You can enter *January* in one cell and used the AutoFill feature to automatically enter the rest of the months.

The **Fill Handle** is the small black square at the lower right of the cell pointer. When you move your mouse pointer over the lower right corner of the active cell, a black plus sign (+) appears. This change is an indication that when you drag the selection down (or to the right), Excel will either copy the contents of the first cell to the selected cells or use it as the first entry in a consecutive series.

So, you first need to click on the cell to select it and then move your mouse pointer over the bottom right corner to display the small plus sign (+).

To AutoFill dates, enter *January* or any other starting month in one cell then grab the small fill handle and drag it across the other cells.

AutoFill also works with abbreviations, but they must be 3 letters. For example, if you enter Jan and then drag down, it will be filled with Feb, Mar, Apr, May etc.

Let's say you want to enter the 7 days of the week as your row headings. In the first cell of your range, enter *Monday* or *Mon*. Then drag the autofill handle down over the remaining 6 cells. This will AutoFill the remaining cells with Tuesday to Sunday.

Excel keeps the filled days selected, giving you a chance to drag the handle back if you went too far, or to drag it further if you didn't go far enough.

You can also use the **AutoFill Options** drop-down menu to further refine your fill options. To access the AutoFill options, with the cells still selected, you will see a drop-down button that appears on the last cell. When you click on it, you will get a list of options that enable you to select whether you want to copy the data across the cells, fill the series, copy formatting only, ignore the formatting, flash fill etc.

Note: If you don't see a button that enables you to access the AutoFill Options drop-down menu (shown above) after an autofill, it is most likely because the option hasn't been set in Excel Options.

To enable AutoFill Options (if it isn't available), navigate to:

1. **File > Options > Advanced**.

2. Under the **Cut, copy, and paste** section, select the checkbox for **Show Paste Options button when content is pasted**.

General	Places: 2
Formulas	☑ Enable fill handle and cell drag-and-drop
	☑ Alert before overwriting cells
Data	☑ Allow editing directly in cells
Proofing	☑ Extend data range formats and formulas
Save	☑ Enable automatic percent entry
Language	☑ Enable AutoComplete for cell values
	☑ Automatically Flash Fill
Ease of Access	☐ Zoom on roll with IntelliMouse
Advanced	☑ Alert the user when a potentially time consuming operation occurs
Customize Ribbon	When this number of cells (in thousands) is affected: 33,554
Quick Access Toolbar	☑ Use system separators
	Decimal separator: .
Add-ins	Thousands separator: ,
Trust Center	Cursor movement:
	◉ Logical
	○ Visual
	☐ Do not automatically hyperlink screenshot

Cut, copy, and paste

☑ Show Paste Options button when content is pasted
☑ Show Insert Options buttons
☑ Cut, copy, and sort inserted objects with their parent cells

Pen

[OK] [Cancel]

AutoFill Incremental Values

To AutoFill other incremental values, you need to first let Excel know what the difference is. So, you would need to enter values in at least two cells before dragging the fill handle across the other cells.

Let's say you want to enter dates that increment by seven days i.e. a weekly interval. You would need to enter two dates (for example, 01/10/19 and 01/17/19). Then you select both cells and drag across the empty cells to autofill the other cells with dates having an interval of 7 days.

You can do the same with other numbers. If you enter 1 and then drag down, the number 1 will just be copied to the other cells. However, if you enter numbers 1 and 2 in two cells, and then select both cells and drag down, you will get 3, 4, 5, 6 etc.

AutoFill Formulas

To AutoFill a formula across several cells enter the formula in the first cell and then drag the fill handle over the other cells in the range. If the cell references are relative, then the references will also change to match the position of the active cell.

For example, if the first cell of your formula is $= A1 + B1$, when you drag this formula down to the other cells, the formula in the other cells will be, $=A2+B2$, $=A3+B3$, $=A4+B4$ and so on.

Another way to use AutoFill is to click on the **Fill** button in the **Editing** group on the **Home** tab.

Note: If the cell references in your formula are absolute, then the cell references will not change when you use AutoFill to copy it to other cells. See the difference between relative and absolute cell references in chapter 6 in this book.

AutoFill the Same Values

To AutoFill the same value across a series of cells, enter the value in the first cell then hold down the **CTRL** key while dragging the fill handle across the other cells.

For example, if you want to fill a range of cells with $6.99:

1. Enter **$6.99** in the first cell.

2. Hold down the **CTRL** key.

3. Move your mouse pointer to the bottom-right of the cell and grab the autofill handle (small square) and then drag it across the other cells.

2.3 Using Flash Fill

Flash Fill is a feature that was introduced in Excel 2013 that enables you to split and rearrange data automatically. In the past, you would need to combine several Excel text functions like LEFT and MID to accomplish the same tasks that you can now do with the Flash Fill command.

For example, if you have a name field (made up of the *first name* and *last name*) that you would like to sort by *last name*. You would need to re-enter the names in another column with the last name first. This is because Excel starts its sorting with the first character of the field, and then the next, and so on.

With Flash Fill, you can insert a new column next to the name column and enter the first value with the last name first. When you enter the second value, Excel will figure out what you're trying to do and automatically Flash Fill the other cells in the format it predicts you want to enter the data. This will save you a lot of time as you only need to enter two cells to have the rest automatically completed for you.

	A	B	C	D	E	F
1						
2			Month 1	Month 2		
3	Jane Smith	Smith, Jane	$1,000.00	$1,100.00		
4	Peter West	West, Peter	$2,000.00	$1,500.00		
5	Derek Brown	Brown, Derek	$1,000.00	$1,200.00		
6	Jason Fields	Fields, Jason	$1,100.00	$1,300.00		
7	Mark Powell	Powell, Mark	$1,500.00	$1,600.00		
8	Julie Rush	Rush, Julie	$1,200.00	$1,300.00		
9						
10						

Steps in Flash Fill:

1. Enter the value in the first cell in the new format.

2. Start entering the second value in the next cell.

3. You'll see a preview of the rest of the column displaying the suggested entries.

4. Press **Enter** to accept the suggestions.

Another way to use Flash Fill is to select **Data > Flash Fill** from the ribbon. The **Flash Fill** command button is in the **Data Tools** group on the **Data** tab.

Insert another column to the right of the one with the original data. Then enter the first value and click on the **Flash Fill** command button. This will automatically enter the rest of the data in the corresponding cells in the same format it was entered in the first cell.

3. DESIGN AND ORGANISE
WORKBOOKS

In this chapter, we'll cover various tasks to do with organising your workbook.

These will include:
- Adding/removing worksheets.
- Moving, copying, hiding and deleting worksheets.
- Freezing rows and columns.
- Applying themes to your worksheets.

3.1 Adding New Worksheets

We covered creating a new workbook in Chapter 1. When you first create a workbook, you'll have one worksheet in it named **Sheet1**.

To add a new sheet to your workbook, click on the plus sign (+) at the bottom of the worksheet area, to the right of Sheet1 and it will create a new worksheet named Sheet2. You can add more worksheets to your workbook this way.

The number of worksheets you can have in a workbook is unlimited. You're only limited by your computer resources like RAM and hard disk space. However, try not to have too many sheets in one workbook as the file can become very large, taking longer to open.

Naming a Worksheet

To name your worksheet, double-click on the name tab at the bottom of the screen and the name will become editable. For example, if you double-click on *Sheet1* the name will be selected with the cursor blinking, allowing you to type in the new name.

3.2 Moving and Copying Worksheets

You can move and reorder your worksheets by clicking on the name and dragging it to the left or right. You can also move a sheet by right-clicking on the name and selecting **Move or Copy** from the pop-up menu.

On the **Move or Copy** screen, select a name from the list and click OK. The selected worksheet will be moved to the front of the sheet selected.

```
Move or Copy                    ?    ✕

Move selected sheets
To book:
┌─────────────────────────────────────┬───┐
│ Excel for beginners.xlsx            │ ∨ │
└─────────────────────────────────────┴───┘
Before sheet:
┌─────────────────────────────────────┬───┐
│ Sheet1                              │ ∧ │
│ Sheet4                              │   │
│ Sheet3                              │   │
│ Sheet2                              │   │
│ Sheet6                              │   │
│ Sheet5                              │   │
│ (move to end)                       │   │
│                                     │ ∨ │
└─────────────────────────────────────┴───┘

☐ Create a copy

        ┌──────────┐    ┌──────────┐
        │    OK    │    │  Cancel  │
        └──────────┘    └──────────┘
```

If you want it copied instead of moved, click on the **Create a copy** checkbox before clicking OK. A copy will be placed in front of the selected sheet.

Removing a Worksheet

On the Sheet tab, right-click the sheet you want to remove and click **Delete**.

If the sheet is empty, it will be deleted right away. If the sheet has data, then you'll get a pop-up message asking you to confirm the deletion. Click on **Delete** to confirm the deletion.

Hide a Worksheet

On the Sheet tab, right-click the sheet you want to hide and select **Hide**.

To unhide a sheet right-click on any of the sheet name tabs. If a sheet is hidden, the **Unhide** option will be available on the pop-up menu. Select **Unhide** to display a window listing the hidden sheets. You can select any sheet on the list and click **OK** to show it again.

3.3 Freezing Rows and Columns

When you have a large worksheet with lots of data, you may want your data headers (row and/or column) to remain visible as you scroll down or to the right of the page.

To make your column headings always visible you can freeze them on the page so that the scroll action does not take them out of view.

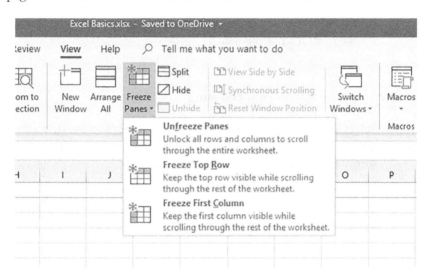

To quickly freeze the top row of your worksheet:

1. Click on the **View** tab on the ribbon.

2. In the Window group click on **Freeze Panes** and select **Freeze Top Row.**

When you now scroll down the page the top row will always remain visible.

To quickly freeze the first column of your worksheet:

1. Click on the **View** tab on the ribbon.

2. In the Window group click on **Freeze Panes** and select **Freeze First Column.**

When you now scroll to the right of the page the first column will always remain visible.

On some occasions, you may want to freeze rows and columns other than the first ones.

To freeze any row of your choosing:

1. Place the cell pointer directly under the row you want to freeze to make it the active cell.

2. Click on the **View** tab.

3. In the Window group click on **Freeze Panes** and select **Freeze Panes** from the pop-up list.

To freeze any column of your choosing:

1. Select a cell on the first row of the column that's to the right of the one you want to freeze. For example, if you want to freeze *column B* then you would select cell *C1*.

2. Click on the **View** tab.

3. In the Window group click on **Freeze Panes** and select **Freeze Panes** from the pop-up list.

Other examples:

*   If you want to freeze the first row and first column of your worksheet, you would select cell **B2** and then select **View** > **Freeze Panes** > **Freeze Panes**.

*   If you want to freeze only rows 1 and 2, you would select cell **A3** and select **View** > **Freeze Panes** > **Freeze Panes**.

*   If you want to freeze only columns A and B, you would click on cell **C1** and select **View** > **Freeze Panes** > **Freeze Panes**.

Unfreeze panes:

To unfreeze any frozen row or columns, click on Freeze Panes and select **Unfreeze Panes** from the pop-up menu.

3.4 Applying Themes to Your Worksheet

A theme is a predefined formatting package that you can apply to your worksheet that may include colours for headers, text fonts, the size of cells etc.

There are several themes in Excel that you can apply to your whole worksheet.

To change the look and feel of your worksheet with themes:

1. Click on the **Page Layout** tab on the Ribbon.

2. Click on the **Themes** button to display the drop-down list with many themes you can apply to your worksheet.

3. You can mouseover a theme on the list to get an instant preview of how your worksheet would look with that theme without selecting it.

4. When you find one that you're happy with, click on it to apply it to your worksheet.

Removing a Theme

If you apply a theme you don't like, simply click the **Undo** button on the Quick Access Toolbar (the left-pointing arrow) to undo the changes and return your worksheet to its previous state.

4. Organising Your Data

Ιn this chapter, we will cover some essential tasks to do with organising your data in Excel.

These will include:
- Copying and pasting data.
- Moving data.
- Inserting/deleting rows and columns.
- Finding and replacing data.
- Sorting data.
- Filtering data.

4.1 Copying, Moving and Deleting Data

Selecting a Group of Cells

Method 1

1. Click on the first cell of the area.

2. Ensure your mouse pointer is a white plus sign.

3. Click and drag over the other cells in the range you want to include in the selection.

Method 2

1. Click on the top-left cell in the range, for example, A2.

2. Hold down the SHIFT key and click on the bottom-right cell in the range, for example, D10.

This will select the range A1:D10.

Deselecting Cells

Sometimes when you're selecting several cells or ranges, you might accidentally select more cells than you intended. You can deselect any extra cells within the selected range with the deselect feature.

To deselect cells within a selection, hold down the **Ctrl** key, then click, or click-and-drag to deselect any cells or ranges within the selection.

If you need to reselect any of the cells, hold down the **Ctrl** key and click on the cells to select them again.

Note: This is a new feature starting from Excel 2019. If you are an Office 365 subscriber, make sure you have the latest version of Office to activate this feature in Excel.

Copying and Pasting Data

Quick copy and paste:

1. Select the range that you want to copy.

2. On the **Home** tab, click on **Copy** (this is the double paper icon next to the Paste command).

3. You will see a dotted line around the area. This is called the marquee.

4. Click on the first cell of the area where you want to paste the contents.

5. Click on **Paste**.

6. The marquee remains active to let you know that you can carry on pasting the copied content if you wish to paste it in multiple areas. To get rid of the marquee hit the **ESC** key.

Other pasting options:

1. To access other pasting options, after copying data, on the toolbar, click the **Paste** command button to display a pop-up menu with several pasting options. You can mouseover the options to see what each one does. You also see a preview of the paste action on your worksheet.

2. For example, if you want to paste the contents and the column width, you would select the option that says **Keep Source Width (W)**. This is on the second row on the menu.

3. Select that option to paste the data as well as the cell formatting and column width.

4. Once done, remove the marquee around the copied range by hitting the ESC key. This tells Excel that you're done with the copying.

Moving Data

To move content, you follow a similar set of actions as we did with copying, however, you would **Cut** the data instead of **Copy** it.

1. Select the range you want to move.

2. On the Home tab, click on the **Cut** button (this is the command with the scissors icon).

3. A scrolling marquee will appear around the area you've chosen to cut.

4. Place your cursor on the first cell of the area where you want to paste the content. You only need to select one cell.

5. Click on **Paste** on your toolbar. This will move the content from its current location and place it in the area you've chosen.

6. The cut and paste action automatically copies the format of the cells across but not the width. So, you need to adjust the width of the cells if necessary.

Insert or Delete Rows and Columns

To insert a column:

1. Click on the column letter immediately to the right of where you want to insert the column. For example, if you want to insert a column between columns A and B, you would select column B.

2. On the **Home** tab, in the Cells group, click the **Insert** button.

This will insert a new column to the left of the one you selected.

Whenever you need to insert a new column, ensure you select the column immediately to the right of the area where you want to insert a new column.

For example, let's say you have data in columns A, B, C and D, and you wish to insert a new column between C and D. You would select column D and then select **Home** > **Insert** to insert a new column between C and D. The new column will now be the new D.

Inserting a new column by using the pop-up menu:

1. Click the column letter to the right of the insertion point to select the whole column.

2. Right-click and select **Insert** from the pop-up menu. This will insert the new column.

Inserting a new row by using the pop-up menu:

1. Click on the row number directly below the insertion point to select the whole row.

2. Right-click and select **Insert** from the pop-up menu. This will insert a new row directly above the selected row.

You could also insert new rows and columns by using the **Insert** command button on the **Home** tab.

Inserting multiple rows or columns:

1. Hold down the CTRL key.

2. One by one, select the rows up to the number you want to insert. For example, if you want to insert 4 rows then select 4 rows directly under the insertion point.

3. Click on **Home > Insert** (or right-click and select **Insert**).

This will insert 4 new rows above the insertion point.

4.2 Find and Replace Data

An Excel worksheet can occasionally be very large. A worksheet can have over a million rows of data, for example, so in a large worksheet, it may be difficult to locate specific information. Excel provides a Find and Replace feature that enables you to quickly find data in your worksheet and replace it if needed.

If you have used the find function in other Microsoft Office applications before, then you should be familiar with this feature.

To display the **Find and Replace** dialogue box, on the **Home** tab of the ribbon, click the **Find & Select** button, and then click on **Find** from the pop-up menu.

The following dialogue box will be displayed.

The **Find what** field contains the value you want to find.

You can click on the **Options** button to display more options to narrow down your search.

1. **Format** allows you to select the format of the data you're searching for.

2. **Within** allows you to search the current worksheet or the whole workbook.

3. **Search** allows you to search by rows (default) or columns.

4. **Look in** is used to search cell formulas, values or comments. The default is formulas so to look for values change this option to Values from the drop-down list.

5. **Match case,** when selected, will only search for values that match the case of the entry in the **Find what** field.

6. **Match entire cell contents,** when selected, ensures that the cell contains the same value as in the **Find what** field.

Replacing Data

To replace data, click on the **Replace** tab of the Find and Replace dialogue. On that tab, you get a **Replace with** field that allows you to enter the data you want to insert in place of what you find.

You get two additional buttons at the bottom of the screen:

1. **Replace All** – Automatically replaces all instances of the Find results.

2. **Replace** – Replace only the next one found.

All the other options on the screen remain the same on this tab.

Tip: If you used **Replace/Replace All** to replace data by mistake you can use the **Undo** button on the Quick Access Toolbar to reverse the changes.

4.3 Sorting Data

Excel offers a wide array of methods to sort your data, from a quick and basic sort to more complex sorts using your own custom list. We will be covering the popular methods in this section.

Quick Sort

To quickly sort data in Excel, select any single cell in the column you want to sort.

Right-click the cell. From the pop-up menu, select **Sort A to Z** (for ascending) or **Sort Z to A** (for descending).

If your column is a number field you'll have, **Sort Smallest to Largest** (for ascending) or **Sort Largest to Smallest** (for descending).

The sort does not change your data in any way. It simply reorders your rows according to the sort order and column you've chosen.

Custom Sort

In the example above, we sorted using just one column. However, you can sort using multiple columns, for example, in the data shown below, we may want to sort by *Category* and *Product name*. In this case, we would use the Custom Sort command on the ribbon.

◢	A	B	C
1	Category	Product Name	Price
2	Beverages	Chai	18.00
3	Condiments	Syrup	10.00
4	Condiments	Cajun Seasoning	22.00
5	Cereal	Granola	4.00
6	Chips, Snacks	Potato Chips	1.80
7	Baked Goods & Mixes	Brownie Mix	12.49
8	Baked Goods & Mixes	Cake Mix	15.99
9	Beverages	Tea	4.00
10	Canned Fruit & Vegetables	Pears	1.30
11	Canned Fruit & Vegetables	Peaches	1.50
12	Canned Fruit & Vegetables	Pineapple	1.80
13	Canned Fruit & Vegetables	Cherry Pie Filling	2.00
14	Canned Fruit & Vegetables	Green Beans	1.20
15	Canned Fruit & Vegetables	Corn	1.20
16	Canned Fruit & Vegetables	Peas	1.50
17	Canned Meat	Tuna Fish	2.00
18	Canned Meat	Smoked Salmon	4.00
19	Cereal	Hot Cereal	5.00
20	Soups	Vegetable Soup	1.89
21	Soups	Chicken Soup	1.95
22			

Applying a custom sort:

Select a single cell anywhere in the data.

On the Home tab, in the Editing group, click **Sort & Filter**, then select **Custom Sort** from the pop-up menu. This will display the Sort dialogue box.

In the **Sort by** list, select the first column you want to sort.

In the **Sort On** list, you have the option of selecting Values, Cell Color, Font Color, or Cell Icon. If you're sorting by value, you'll leave this as the default (Value).

In the **Order** list, select the order in which you want to sort. For a text column, you can choose **A to Z** (ascending order) or **Z to A** (descending order).

For a number column, you can choose **Smallest to Largest** or **Largest to Smallest**.

Click **OK** when you're done.

Your data will now be sorted according to the criteria you've entered.

Sorting with a Custom List

When you click in the **Order** list, you can also select **Custom List** from the drop-down list and sort data by days of the week or months. You can add your own list (if the pre-defined ones do not meet your needs). This is useful when you want to sort using your own custom order rather than the standard ascending or descending order.

Custom Lists	? X

Custom Lists

Custom lists:

NEW LIST	Higher Executive Officer
Mon, Tue, Wed, Thu, Fri, Sat, S	Executive Officer
Monday, Tuesday, Wednesday,	Admin Officer
Jan, Feb, Mar, Apr, May, Jun, Jt	Admin Assistant
January, February, March, Apri	
Westminister, Oxford, Piccadill	

List entries:

Add

Delete

Press Enter to separate list entries.

OK   Cancel

For example, if we wanted to sort our data by *employee grade* we could enter the grades in our list in the order we want the data sorted.

To add a new custom list, select NEW LIST in the left box. In the **List entries** box on the right, enter the items one item per line.

When you're done, click the **Add** button to add the list. You can now select the list and click **OK** to use it for your sort.

Your custom list will now be available to all Excel workbooks on the PC.

4.4 Filtering Data

Excel worksheets can hold a lot of data and you might not want to work with all the data at the same time. For example, you might want to only display a category of products or products within a certain price range.

Excel 2019 provides an array of options to filter your data so that you can only view data that meets a certain criterion. Filters provide a quick way to work with a subset of data in a range or table. When you apply the filter, you temporarily hide some of the data so that you can focus on the data you need to work with.

Excel tables would have column headings by default, however, if your data is not an Excel table, ensure you have column headings, like Category, Product Name, Price etc. This makes using sort much easier.

	Category	Product Name	Price	Reorder Level	Target Level
1	Category	Product Name	Price	Reorder Level	Target Level
2	Beverages	Chai	18.00	10	40
3	Condiments	Syrup	10.00	25	100
4	Condiments	Cajun Seasoning	22.00	10	40
5	Oil	Olive Oil	21.35	10	40
6	Jams, Preserves	Boysenberry Spread	25.00	25	100
7	Dried Fruit & Nuts	Dried Pears	30.00	10	40
8	Sauces	Curry Sauce	40.00	10	40

You can add column headings to your data by inserting a new row at the top of your worksheet and entering the headings. This is important because Excel will use the first row for the filter arrows.

How to filter data:

1. Select any cell within the data that you want to filter.

2. Click on **Home > Sort & Filter > Filter** (or click **Data > Filter**).

3. You will get a **filter arrow** at the top of each column. This is also called an **AutoFilter**. Note that in Excel tables, filter arrows are turned on by default.

4. Click the AutoFilter of the column you want to filter. For example, Price.

5. Uncheck **Select All** and check the values you want to use for the filter.

6. Click **OK.**

	A	B	C	D	E	
1	Product Code	Product Name	Price	Reorder Level	Category	
16	NWTSO-41	Clam Chowder	$9.65	10	Soups	
17	NWTB-43	Coffee	$46.00	25	Beverages	
18	NWTCA-48	Chocolate	$12.75	25	Candy	
19	NWTDFN-51	Dried Apples	$53.00	10	Dried Fruit & Nuts	
20	NWTG-52	Long Grain Rice	$7.00	25	Grains	
21	NWTP-56	Gnocchi	$38.00	30	Pasta	
22	NWTP-57	Ravioli	$19.50	20	Pasta	
23	NWTS-65	Hot Pepper Sauce	$21.05	10	Sauces	
24	NWTS-66	Tomato Sauce	$17.00	20	Sauces	
25	NWTD-72	Mozzarella	$34.80	10	Dairy Products	
26	NWTDFN-74	Almonds	$10.00	5	Dried Fruit & Nuts	
27	NWTCO-77	Mustard	$13.00	15	Condiments	
28	NWTDFN-80	Dried Plums	$3.50	50	Dried Fruit & Nuts	
29	NWTB-81	Green Tea	$2.99	100	Beverages	
30	NWTC-82	Granola	$4.00	20	Cereal	

The AutoFilter changes to a funnel icon to show that the column is filtered. If you look at the row heading numbers, you'll see that they're now blue, indicating which rows are included in the filtered data.

Applying a Custom Filter

Click on the AutoFilter of the column you want to use for the filter.

On the pop-up menu, you'll get a menu item and a pop-out menu. You'll get the following options depending on the datatype of the column:

1. **Text Filters** - this is available when the column has a text field or has a mixture of text and numbers: Equals, Does Not Equal, Begins With, Ends With, or Contains.

2. **Number Filters** - this option is only available when the column contains only numbers: Equals, Does Not Equal, Greater Than, Less Than, or Between.

3. **Date Filters** - this option is only available when the column contains only dates: Last Week, Next Month, This Month, and Last Month.

4. **Clear Filter from 'Column name'** - this option is only available if a filter has already been applied to the column. Select this option to clear the filter.

When you select any of the first 3 options you will get a dialogue box – **Custom AutoFilter**. You'll be specifying your custom filter conditions using this screen.

For example, if you wanted to display data with a price range between $2 and $10, you would:

1. Click on the **Price** AutoFilter and then select **Number Filters** > **Between...** from the pop-up menu.

	▼ Product Name	▼ Price	▼ Reorder Leve ▼	Target Level ▼
↑Z↓	Sort Smallest to Largest		10	40
↓Z↑	Sort Largest to Smallest		25	100
	Sort by Color ▶		10	40
✗	Clear Filter From "Price"		10	40
	Filter by Color ▶		25	100
	Number Filters ▶		10	40

Number Filters submenu:
- Equals...
- Does Not Equal...
- Greater Than...
- Greater Than Or Equal To...
- Less Than...
- Less Than Or Equal To...
- Between...
- Top 10...
- Above Average
- Below Average
- Custom Filter...

Search [🔍]
- ☑ (Select All)
- ☑ 1.20
- ☑ 1.30
- ☑ 1.50
- ☑ 1.80
- ☑ 1.89
- ☑ 1.95
- ☑ 2.00
- ☑ 2.99
- ☑ 3.50

[OK] [Cancel]

bles

The **Custom AutoFilter** screen allows you to enter the criteria and specify the condition.

Custom AutoFilter   ? ✕

Show rows where:
Price

is greater than or equal to ∨ $2

○ And ○ Or

is less than or equal to ∨ $10

Use ? to represent any single character
Use * to represent any series of characters

[OK] [Cancel]

2. Enter the values you want to use for the filter. In our example, the values would be $2 and $10.

3. Select the logical operator. In this case, we'll need **And**, as both conditions must be true.

   Price >= $2 And <= $10. If only one of either condition needs to be true, then you would select Or.

4. Click OK when done.

The data will now be filtered to only show records where the Price is between $2 and $10.

Changing the Sort Order of a Filtered List

To change the sort order of the filtered results, click the **AutoFilter** icon that appears on the column used for the filter.

Select either, **Sort Largest to Smallest** or **Sort Smallest to Largest**. For a text column, it would be **Sort A to Z** or **Sort Z to A.**

Removing a Filter

Select any cell in the range/table and click on **Clear** in the **Sort & Filter** group. The filter will be removed, and all data will be displayed.

5. FORMATTING CELLS

In this chapter, we will cover various methods to format and resize cells in your worksheet to present your data in your desired format.

The topics covered will include, how to:
- Resize cells, rows, and columns.
- Hide and unhide rows and columns.
- Merge cells and align data.
- Hide and unhide worksheets.
- Apply predefined cell styles.
- Apply different types of number formats to cells.
- Create and apply custom cell formats.
- Apply conditional formatting to add visual representations to your data.

5.1 Arrange Cells, Rows and Columns

Resizing Rows and Columns

You can resize rows and columns with your mouse or by using the **Format** command on the toolbar.

To resize a column:

1. Click on any cell in the column.

2. Click on the right edge of the column letter and drag it to the right to widen the column.

To resize a row:

1. Click on any cell in the row.

2. Click on the bottom edge of the row number then drag it down to increase the height of the row.

Resizing Cells with the Cells Format Command

You can also increase column width and row height of a range of cells at once by using the **Format** command button on the **Home** tab of the ribbon.

To increase the widths of columns A to E, for example:

1. Move your mouse pointer over the letter A until you see a downward pointing arrow.

2. Click on A to select the column and drag to column E to select columns A to E.

   Tip: Another way to select a range of columns is to select the first column, hold down the SHIFT key, and select the last column.

3. Click on **Home > Format > Column Width**.

4. Enter the **Column width** in the box.

5. Click **OK**.

To increase the height of rows 1 to 14, for example:

1. Move your mouse pointer over the header of row 1 until you get an arrow pointing right.

2. Click to select the whole row.

3. Hold down the SHIFT key and click on the header of row 14.

4. Click on **Home > Format > Row Height...**

5. The default row height is 15. So, you can enter any number higher than 15 to increase the height of the selected rows.

6. Click **OK**.

Automatically adjust columns to fit your data using AutoFit

Select the columns you want to apply AutoFit to. Click on **Format > AutoFit Column Width**. This will adjust each column to fit the length of all entries.

Automatically adjust row heights to fit your data using AutoFit

Select the rows you want to apply AutoFit to. Select **Format** > **AutoFit Row Height**. This will adjust each column to fit the height of all entries. This is useful if you have **Wrap text** enabled and some cells have more than one line of text.

Set the default column width for the whole workbook

Select **Format** > **Default Width** and then enter the figure in the **Standard column width** box.

Hide Rows and Columns

On some occasions, you may want to hide some rows or columns to make your worksheet easier to read.

To hide **rows,** select the rows and then click on **Format**. On the pop-up menu, under **Visibility**, select **Hide & Unhide** and then select **Hide Rows**.

To hide **columns**, select the columns and then click on **Format**. On the pop-up menu, under **Visibility**, select **Hide & Unhide** and then select **Hide Columns**.

Unhide rows and columns:

Navigate to **Home** > **Format** > **Hide & Unhide** and then select **Unhide Columns** to display hidden columns (or **Unhide Rows** to display hidden rows).

Hide and Unhide a Worksheet

You can use two methods to hide a worksheet:

Method 1: Right-click on the worksheet's name tab and select **Hide** from the pop-up menu.

Method 2: Ensure the worksheet you want to hide is the active one, then select **Home > Format > Hide & Unhide > Hide Sheet**.

To Unhide a worksheet:

Method 1: Right-click on any of the tabs at the bottom of the workbook and select **Unhide** from the pop-up menu. Select the worksheet name in the **Unhide** window and click **OK**.

Method 2: Navigate to **Home > Format > Hide & Unhide > Unhide Sheet**. Select the sheet name from the list box and click **OK**.

Applying Cell Styles

You can select a predefined colour format for your cells from a wide selection of styles from the **Styles** group on the **Home** tab.

To format a cell or range with a different style:

- Select the cell or range.

- Select **Home > Cell Styles**.

- You can mouseover the different styles to get a preview on your worksheet before you select one.

- Select a style from the pop-up menu.

Merging Cells and Aligning Data

To **merge** cells on your worksheet, select the cells you want to merge. On the **Home** tab, click **Merge & Center**. Alternatively, you can click on the drop-down button for Merge & Center and choose other merge options from the pop-up menu.

To **unmerge** cells, select the merged cells, then on the **Home** tab, click on the drop-down button for **Merge & Center**. Select **Unmerge Cells** from the pop-up menu.

Text Alignment and Wrapping

To align text in a cell, select the cell and click on one of the alignment options in the **Alignment** group on the **Home** tab. You can also wrap text and merge cells from the command options available.

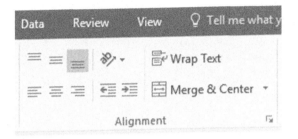

Shrink to Fit and Text Direction

The **Format Cells** dialogue box provides additional formatting options like **Shrink to fit** and **Text direction**. To open the dialogue box, click on the dialogue box launcher on the bottom-right of the **Alignment** group.

Format Cells	? ✕

Number **Alignment** Font Border Fill Protection

Text alignment

Horizontal:

[_____] ▾ Indent:

Vertical:

Bottom ▾ [___] ▴▾

☐ Justify distributed

Text control

☐ Wrap text
☐ Shrink to fit
☐ Merge cells

Right-to-left

Text direction:

Context ▾

Orientation

T e x t   Text ⟶ ◆

0 ▴▾ Degrees

[OK] [Cancel]

On the Alignment tab, you can:

1. Align text in your cells vertically and horizontally.

2. Wrap text so that it goes to a new line in a cell instead of continuing into other cells to the right.

3. Shrink text to fit one cell.

4. Merge cells.

5.2 Applying Number Formats

To quickly set the format for a range of cells:

1. Select the range of cells that you want to format.

2. On the **Home** tab, locate the **Number** group and click the drop-down list to display a number of formats.

3. Select one of the formats from the list, for example, Currency, Short Date or Time.

The selected cell/range will now be formatted in the format you selected.

Accessing More Formats

To choose a format that is not on the format drop-down list, for example, if you're in the US and you want to change the currency from US dollars to UK pounds:

1. Select **More Number Formats...** at the bottom of the drop-down list (shown above) or click on the **dialog box launcher** (the small diagonal arrow at the bottom-right of the **Number** group).

    The **Format Cells** window will be displayed.

2. On the left side of the dialogue box under **Category**, select **Currency**.

3. Click on the **Symbol** field to display a drop-down list. Select the British pound sign (£) from the list.

    On this screen, you can also set the number of decimal places and the format you want for negative numbers. The **Sample** field gives you a preview of how the chosen format will look on your worksheet.

4. Click **OK** to confirm your changes when done.

Creating Custom Numeric Formats

Excel has many predefined number formats you can select and then amend, to create your own custom format if none of the predefined formats meets your needs.

Let's say you have a column in your worksheet that you use to record a set of numbers. It could be product serial numbers, unique product IDs, or even telephone numbers. You may want the numbers to appear in a certain format regardless of how they've been entered.

In some applications like Microsoft Access, this would be called a *format mask*.

In Excel, you can create your own format for a group of cells, so that every entry is automatically formatted with your default format.

To create your own format:

1. Select the range of cells to be formatted.

2. Right-click any area in your selection and choose **Format Cells** from the pop-up menu. Alternatively, launch the **Format Cells** window by clicking the dialog box launcher in the **Number** group on the **Home** tab.

3. Under **Category,** select **Custom.**

4. In the **Type** box, select an existing format close to the one you would like to create.

   Note: If you find a format on the list that meets your needs then you can just select that one and click OK.

5. In the Type box, type in the format you want to create. For example, *0000-00000.*

6. Click **OK**.

◢	A	B	C
1	**Serial Number**		
2	234401107	2344-01107	
3	234434589	2344-34589	
4	234466123	2344-66123	
5	234455692	2344-55692	
6	234234500	2342-34500	
7	234410976	2344-10976	
8	232310978	2323-10978	
9	234093419	2340-93419	
10	230923100	2309-23100	
11	234109035	2341-09035	
12	234102345	2341-02345	
13	234109093	2341-09093	
14			

In the image above, column A has a set of numbers. Column B shows the same numbers with a custom format (*0000-00000*) now applied to them.

5.3 Copy Cell Formatting

A quick way to format a cell or group of cells based on another cell is to use the **Format Painter**. This can be found in the **Clipboard** group on the **Home** tab. This can save a lot of time as you only create the format once and copy it to other cells in your worksheet for which you would like to apply that format.

To copy cell formatting with the Format Painter:

1. Click on the source cell, that is the cell you want to copy the format from.

2. Select **Home > Format Painter**. The mouse pointer will turn into a plus sign (+) and a brush icon.

3. Click and drag over the destination cells i.e. the cells you want to copy the format to. The destination cells will now have the same format as the source cell.

An Example:

If cell A2 is formatted as **Currency** and you want to format A3 to A14 as currency with the **Format Painter**, you would carry out the following steps:

1. Click on cell *A2* to select it.

2. Click on **Format Painter**.

3. Select *A3* to *A14*. Click *A3* and drag to *A14*.

4. The currency format from *A2* will now be applied to A3:A14.

Clearing the Cell Format

To remove formatting from a cell or range, do the following:

1. Select the cells you want to clear.

2. Select **Home > Clear** (from the **Editing** group).

3. A pop-up menu with several options will be displayed - **Clear All, Clear Formats, Clear Contents, Clear Comments, and Clear Hyperlinks**.

4. To clear just the format and not the values, click on **Clear Formats**.

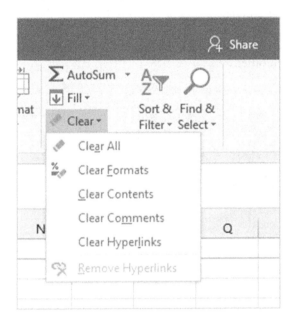

This will return the format of the selected cells to **General** which is the Excel default.

5.4 Conditional Formatting

With conditional formatting, you can format your data based on certain conditions to display a visual representation that helps you to spot critical issues and to identify patterns and trends. For example, you can use visual representations to clearly show the highs and lows in your data, and the trend based on a set of criteria.

In the example below, we can quickly see the trend in sales and how they compare to each other.

	A	B	C	D	E	
1	Month	Sales			Product Code	Pro
2	Jan	$4,200.00			5145	Cha
3	Feb	$2,100.00			6254	Syr
4	Mar	$3,400.00			1448	Caj
5	Apr	$4,200.00			5881	Oliv
6	May	$3,810.50			7009	Boy
7	Jun	$5,500.00			5321	Drie
8	Jul	$3,400.00			2863	Cur
9	Aug	$7,100.00			2446	Wal
10	Sep	$4,105.00			1665	Frui
11	Oct	$8,000.00			9570	Cho
12	Nov	$8,400.00			5430	Mar
13	Dec	$10,000.00			3849	Sco
14						
15						
16						
17						
18						
19						
20						
21						
22						

Formatting	Charts	Totals	Tables	Sparklines
Data Bars	Color...	Icon Set	Greater...	Top 10%	Clear...

Conditional Formatting uses rules to highlight interesting data.

To quickly apply a conditional format:

1. Select the range of cells you want to format.

    The quick analysis button will be displayed at the bottom-right of the selection.

2. Click the Quick Analysis button, and use the default **Formatting** tab.

3. When you mouseover the formatting options, you'll see a live preview of what your data will look like when applied.

4. Click on **Data Bars** (or any of the other options) to apply the formatting to your data.

You now have a visual representation of the data that's easier to analyze.

Use Multiple Conditional Formats

You can apply more than one conditional format to the same group of cells. To do so, select the cells, click the Quick Analysis button, and click another format option, for example, Icon Set. The arrows are used to depict the upper, middle, and lower values in the set of data.

Formatting Text Fields

You can also apply conditional formatting to text, however, the formatting options for text are different from that of numbers.

For example, to if we wanted to highlight all the rows with "Sauce" in the name, we would...

1. Select the range.

2. Click the Quick Analysis button.

3. Select **Text...** from the Formatting options.

4. In the **Text That Contains** dialogue, we would enter *Sauce* in the first box and select the type of formatting we want from the drop-down list.

	E	F	G	H	I	J
Product Code	Product Name					
5384	Chai					
4567	Syrup					
5459	Cajun Seasoning					
1782	Olive Oil					
1130	Boysenberry Spread					
3080	Dried Pears					
1604	Curry Sauce					
2108	Salad Sauce					
1877	Fruit Cocktail					
8454	Chocolate Biscuits Mix					
9521	Marmalade					
4684	Pepper Sauce					

Text That Contains ? ✕

Format cells that contain the text:

Sauce	⬆	with	Light Red Fill with Dark Red Text ⌄

OK   Cancel

You can explore the formatting options for different data types by selecting the data to be formatted and clicking on the Quick Analysis button.

Conditionally Formatting Time

Let's say we had a task list and we wanted to see which ones are late, i.e. the ones with the due date before today.

1. Select the cells in the *Due date* column.

2. Click the Quick Analysis button, and then click Less Than.

3. Type in **=TODAY()**

    We could type in today's date, but that would mean we would need to update the conditional formatting daily, and that could get tedious fast! The TODAY function will always return today's date.

4. Select the formatting you'll like to use from the drop-down list.

5. Click **OK**.

◢	A	B	C	D	E	F	G	H	I	J
1	Task	Due Date								
2	Task 1	01/23/2018								
3	Task 2	02/21/2018								
4	Task 3	12/03/2017								
5	Task 4	12/04/2017	Less Than					?	×	
6	Task 5	11/05/2017								
7	Task 6	12/30/2017	Format cells that are LESS THAN:							
8	Task 7	12/25/2017	=TODAY()			↑	with	Light Red Fill with Dark Red Text	∨	
9	Task 8	03/01/2018								
10	Task 9	12/01/2017					OK		Cancel	
11	Tast 10	01/30/2018								
12										

The tasks that are overdue now stand out in the list and are easy to identify at a glance.

Creating Conditional Formatting Rules

An alternative way to create conditional formatting is by creating Rules in Excel.

To launch the **New Formatting Rule** dialogue:

1. Select the range you want to apply the conditional formatting to.

2. On the ribbon, click on **Home > Conditional Formatting > New Rule**.

New Formatting Rule	?	X

Select a Rule Type:

> ↦ Format all cells based on their values
> ↦ Format only cells that contain
> ↦ Format only top or bottom ranked values
> ↦ Format only values that are above or below average
> ↦ Format only unique or duplicate values
> ↦ Use a formula to determine which cells to format

Edit the Rule Description:

Format all cells based on their values:

Format Style: | 2-Color Scale | ∨ |

	Minimum			Maximum	
Type:	Lowest Value	∨		Highest Value	∨
Value:	(Lowest value)	⬆		(Highest value)	⬆
Color:		∨			∨
Preview:					

OK	Cancel

You can use this dialogue to create more complex rules using a series of conditions and criteria.

You can select a rule type from the following options:

1. Format all cells based on their values.

2. Format only cells that contain.

3. Format only top or bottom ranked values.

4. Format only values that are above or below average.

5. Format only unique or duplicate values.

6. Use a formula to determine which cells to format.

For each rule type, the bottom half of the screen, labelled **Edit the Rule Description**, gives you different fields to define your rule.

Example:

Let's say you had a products table and you wanted to format the whole row grey if the product stock fell below 10.

To do this, you select the range you want to conditionally format i.e. A2:C18. Note that A2 is the active cell.

On the ribbon, you click **Conditional Formatting** > **New Rule** and select *Use a formula to determine which cells to format.*

	A	B	C	D	E	F	G	H
1	**Product Name**	**Price**	**Stock**					
2	Brownie Mix	$2.49	11					
3	Cake Mix	$1.59	7					
4	Chai	$1.80	16					
5	Tea	$1.50	9					
6	Cherry Pie Filling	$2.00	65					
7	Corn	$1.20	33					
8	Green Beans	$1.20	3					
9	Peaches	$1.50	81					
10	Pears	$1.30	36					
11	Peas	$1.50	5					
12	Pineapple	$1.80	24					
13	Smoked Salmon	$4.00	1					
14	Tuna Fish	$2.00	9					
15	Granola	$4.00	61					
16	Hot Cereal	$5.00	31					
17	Potato Chips	$1.80	10					
18	Cajun Seasoning	$2.00	1					
19								

New Formatting Rule ? ✕

Select a Rule Type:

- Format all cells based on their values
- Format only cells that contain
- Format only top or bottom ranked values
- Format only values that are above or below average
- Format only unique or duplicate values
- Use a formula to determine which cells to format

Edit the Rule Description:

Format values where this formula is true:

=$C2 < 10

Preview: AaBbCcYyZz   Format...

OK   Cancel

Since A2 is the active cell, you need to enter a formula that is valid for row 2 and will apply to all the other rows.

To do this, you type in the formula =$C2 < 10. The dollar sign before the C means it is an **absolute reference** for column C ($C). With this, the value in column C for each row is evaluated and used for the conditional formatting.

Note: The difference between an absolute reference and a relative reference is covered in chapter 6.

For the fill colour, click the **Format** button, select the fill colour you want and click OK and OK again to apply the rule.

The rows with Stock below 10 will now be filled with grey.

	A	B	C	D
1	**Product Name**	**Price**	**Stock**	
2	Brownie Mix	$2.49	11	
3	Cake Mix	$1.59	7	
4	Chai	$1.80	16	
5	Tea	$1.50	9	
6	Cherry Pie Filling	$2.00	65	
7	Corn	$1.20	33	
8	Green Beans	$1.20	3	
9	Peaches	$1.50	81	
10	Pears	$1.30	36	
11	Peas	$1.50	5	
12	Pineapple	$1.80	24	
13	Smoked Salmon	$4.00	1	
14	Tuna Fish	$2.00	9	
15	Granola	$4.00	61	
16	Hot Cereal	$5.00	31	
17	Potato Chips	$1.80	10	
18	Cajun Seasoning	$2.00	1	
19				

6. CARRYING OUT CALCULATIONS WITH FORMULAS

E xcel provides tools and features that enable you to carry out different types of calculations from basic arithmetic to complex engineering calculations using functions.

In this chapter we will cover:

- Operator precedence in Excel and it's effect on calculations.
- How to enter formulas in Excel.
- How to calculate percentages, dates and time.
- How to use the AutoSum feature for automated calculations.
- The difference between relative and absolute cell references.
- How to access data in other worksheets in your formulas.

6.1 Operators in Excel

Arithmetic Operators

The following arithmetic operators are used to perform basic mathematical operations such as addition, subtraction, multiplication, or division.

Arithmetic operator	Meaning	Example
+ (plus sign)	Addition	=4+4
– (minus sign)	Subtraction Negation	=4–4 =-4
* (asterisk)	Multiplication	=4*4
/ (forward slash)	Division	=4/4
% (percent sign)	Percent	40%
^ (caret)	Exponentiation	=4^4

Comparison Operators

Comparison operators allow you to compare two values and produce a logical result i.e. TRUE or FALSE.

Comparison operator	Meaning	Example
=	Equal to	=A1=B1
>	Greater than	=A1>B1
<	Less than	=A1<B1
>=	Greater than or equal to	=A1>=B1
<=	Less than or equal to	=A1<=B1
<>	Not equal to	=A1<>B1

Operator Precedence

If you combine several operators in a single formula, Excel performs the operations in the following order.

Operator	Description
: (colon) (single space) ,(comma)	Reference operators
−	Negation (as in –1)
%	Percent
^	Exponentiation
* and /	Multiplication and division
+ and −	Addition and subtraction
&	Connects two strings of text (concatenation)
= < > <= >= <>	Comparison

At a basic level, you just need to remember that multiplication and division are carried out before addition and subtraction.

If a formula contains operators with the same precedence, for example, multiplication and division, Excel evaluates the operators from left to right.

Parentheses and Operator Precedence

You can change the order of evaluation by enclosing parts of your formula in parentheses (). The part of the formula in parentheses will be calculated first.

For example, the following formula produces 75 because Excel calculates multiplication before addition. So, Excel multiplies 7 by 10 first before adding 5 to the result.

=5+7*10

Answer = 75

In contrast, if we enclose 5+7 in parentheses, Excel will calculate 5 + 7 first before multiplying the result by 7 to produce 120.

=(5+7)*10

Answer = 120

In another example, we want to add 20% to 300. The parentheses around the second part of the formula makes Excel carry out the addition first before the multiplication to produce 360.

=300 * (1 + 0.2)

Answer = 360

6.2 Entering a Formula

To enter a formula in a cell, always start your entry with an equal sign (=) in the formula bar. This tells Excel that your entry is a formula and not a static value.

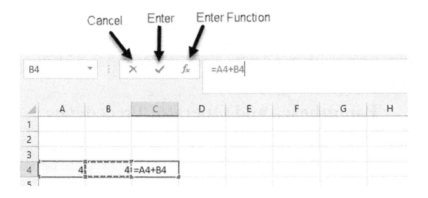

Next to the formula bar, you have the **Enter** command (check mark) that you use to confirm your formula. So, you enter your formula in the formula bar and then click on **Enter** to confirm the entry. If you wish to cancel the entry, then click on **Cancel** to discard it.

Let's say we want to add 2 figures, 300 + 400.

1. Enter 300 in cell **A4**.

2. Enter 400 in cell **B4**.

3. In cell C4, enter $= A4 + B4$.

4. Click on **Enter**.

5. C4 will now have the sum of the two figures which is 700.

Tip: To minimise the possibility of errors, as much as possible, avoid typing cell references directly into the formula bar. After you type in the leading equal sign (=) in the formula bar, you can add cell references to your formula by selecting them on the worksheet with your mouse. Whenever you want to reference a cell, select the cell on the worksheet with your mouse to automatically enter its reference in the formula bar.

So, for the basic calculation we carried out above, the way you would enter it in the formula bar is as follows:

1. Select *C4*

2. Type "=" in the formula bar

3. Select on *A4*

4. Type "+"

5. Select *B4*

6. Click **Enter**

The sum of the 2 cells, i.e. 700, will now be displayed in cell C4.

6.3 Calculating Percentages

Let's say we want to calculate 20% of a value and then add it to the total, the way sales tax is calculated in invoices.

The price of the product is $2,900 and the sales tax is 20%.

Note: 100 percent is 1 in Excel, so, anything less than 100 percent will be less than 1. Hence, 20 percent will be 0.2. Always enter a percent as a decimal place number, unless it is 100% or greater.

For the **Sales tax,** we then enter 0.2 in cell B3.

We can format the cell as a **Percentage** (although this is not a must when calculating percentages in Excel). On the Home tab, in the Numbers group, click on the % sign. This will change the 0.2 to 20%.

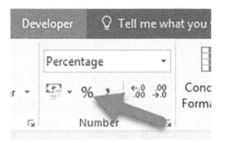

For the **Price**, enter $2,900.

For the Sales Tax formula, enter *=A6*B3* to calculate 20% of $2,900, which is $580.00.

For the **Total**, you can use the AutoSum tool to generate the sum, or you can enter the formula directly *=SUM(A6:B6)* to produce the total figure of $3,480.00.

| B6 | ▼ | ⋮ | × | ✓ | *fx* | =A6*B3 |

	A	B	C	D
1	Calculating percentages			
2				
3	Sales tax rate:	20%		
4				
5	Price	Sales Tax	Total	
6	$2,900.00	$580.00	$3,480.00	
7				

You can use the same method above to subtract percentages. For example, if we wanted to subtract the Sales Tax from the Price we would enter *=A6-B6* in cell c6.

6.4 The AutoSum Tool

The AutoSum tool can be found on the **Home** tab of the ribbon. It is the Greek Sigma symbol in the **Editing** group. AutoSum allows you to insert functions in your worksheet. The tool automatically selects the range to be used as the argument for you. You can use AutoSum with the SUM, AVERAGE, COUNT, MAX, and MIN functions.

AutoSum will default to the SUM function when clicked. However, you can use a different function with AutoSum by clicking the drop-down button next to the AutoSum sign to display a pop-up menu of the other functions you can use. Click on one of them, for example, **Average**, to insert that as the function to be used with AutoSum.

A *range* in Excel is a collection of two or more cells that contain the data you're working with. See chapter 8 for more on ranges.

A function *argument* is a piece of data that a function needs to run. The SUM function, for example, can have one or more arguments for the input ranges to be summed.

=SUM(A2:A10)

=SUM(A2:A10, C2:C10)

The great thing about AutoSum is that it selects the most likely range of cells in the current column or row that you want to use. It then automatically enters them in the function's argument.

For the most part, it selects the correct range of cells and marks the selection with a moving dotted line called the *marquee*. On occasions where there are blank rows or columns in your data, i.e. the data is not continuous, AutoSum may not automatically select everything. In those cases, you can manually correct the range by dragging the cell pointer over the other cells you want in the formula.

Let's say we have figures in B2 to B13 that we want to sum up. We can do so quickly using the AutoSum command.

SUM	▼ ⋮	✕ ✓ *fx*	=SUM(B2:B13)

	A	B	C	D	E
1	**Month**	**Expenses**			
2	Jan	$400.00			
3	Feb	$500.00			
4	Mar	$300.00			
5	Apr	$700.00			
6	May	$800.00			
7	Jun	$750.00			
8	Jul	$800.00			
9	Aug	$600.00			
10	Sep	$550.00			
11	Oct	$420.00			
12	Nov	$350.00			
13	Dec	$800.00			
14	**Sum**	=SUM(B2:B13)			
15		SUM(**number1**, [number2], ...)			
16					

1. Click on the cell where you want the total displayed. For this example, this would be **B14**.

2. Click the **AutoSum** command button (**Home** > **Editing** group > **AutoSum**).

3. AutoSum will automatically select the range of cells with continuous data (above or to the side of the cell with the formula). In this case, it selects B2 to B13.

4. Click **Enter** (the check mark next to the formula bar) or hit the **Enter** key.

Cell B14 will now show the sum of the numbers.

Using AutoSum with Non-contiguous data

A non-contiguous range has blank rows or columns in the data. AutoSum will only select the contiguous range next to the cell with the formula. So, you have to manually drag the selection over the rest of the data.

1. Click on the cell where you want the total to be displayed.

2. Click the **AutoSum** command button.

3. AutoSum will automatically select the range of cells next to the cell with the formula.

4. Place your mouse pointer at the edge of the selection (over the cell pointer) until it turns into a double-headed arrow. Drag it over the rest of the cells in your range.

5. Click the **Enter** button or hit the **Enter** key on your keyboard.

The formula cell will now show the sum of the numbers.

| B17 | ▾ | ⋮ | ✕ | ✓ | ƒx | =SUM(B2:B16) |

◢	A	B	C	D	E
1	Month	Expenses			
2	Jan	$400.00			
3	Feb	$500.00			
4	Mar	$300.00			
5					
6	Apr	$700.00			
7	May	$800.00			
8	Jun	$750.00			
9					
10	Jul	$800.00			
11	Aug	$600.00			
12	Sep	$550.00			
13					
14	Oct	$420.00			
15	Nov	$350.00			
16	Dec	$800.00			
17	Sum	=SUM(B2:B16)			
18		SUM(number1, [number2], ...)			

Cell pointer

Using AutoSum with Different Ranges

Sometimes the data you want to calculate may be in different parts of your worksheet or even on different sheets in the workbook. With AutoSum, you can have arguments for individual values, cell references, ranges, or a mix of all three. So, to calculate different ranges you place the ranges as different arguments.

Summing up values in different ranges:

1. Click on the cell where you want the formula and then click on **AutoSum**.

2. If AutoSum does not select the first range for you then select it by clicking on the first cell and dragging to the last cell of the range.

3. Hold down the **CTRL** key and select any additional ranges you want to add to the calculation.

4. Click **Enter**.

D3		▾	⋮	✕	✓	f_x	=SUM(B3:B8,D3:D8)

⊿	A	B	C	D	E	F	G
1							
2		**Month 1**		**Month 2**			
3	Jane	$1,000.00		$1,100.00			
4	Peter	$2,000.00		$1,500.00			
5	Derek	$1,000.00		$1,200.00			
6	Jason	$1,100.00		$1,300.00			
7	Mark	$1,500.00		$1,600.00			
8	Julie	$1,200.00		$1,300.00			
9							
10							
11	Total			=SUM(B3:B8,D3:D8			
12				SUM(number1, **[number2]**, [number3], …)			
13							

The sum of both ranges will now be entered. You can include up to 255 ranges as arguments in your SUM function.

Using AutoSum for Other Aggregate Functions

As mentioned previously, despite the name, you can use the AutoSum feature to also calculate the **Average, Count, Max,** and **Min.** To select these other functions, click on the drop-down arrow on the AutoSum command and select one of them.

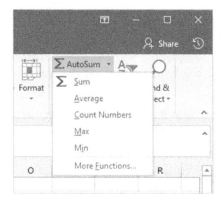

For example, to calculate the average of a row of numbers in cells B4 to I4, you would do the following:

1. Place the cell pointer in the cell where you want to display the average. This will be J4 for this example.

2. Click on **AutoSum** > **Average**.

3. AutoSum will automatically select all the contiguous cells next to the formula cell. For this example, it will be B4 to I4.

4. Click on **Enter** or press the **Enter** key.

DATE		▼		×	✓	fx	=AVERAGE(B4:I4)				
	A	B	C	D	E	F	G	H	I	J	K	L
1	Expenses											
2												
3		Total										
4	Jan	$177.90	$22.40	$33.70	$44.90	$21.90	$22.00	$10.00	$23.00	=AVERAGE(B4:I4)		
5	Feb	$245.00	$33.00	$32.00	$41.00	$31.00	$42.00	$11.00	$55.00	AVERAGE(number1, [number2] ...)		
6	Mar	$281.00	$60.00	$21.00	$30.00	$55.00	$60.00	$22.00	$33.00			
7	Apr											
8	May											
9	Jun											

The average for B4:I4 will now be calculated and displayed in J4.

6.5 Quick Sum with the Status Bar

If you want to quickly see the sum of a range of cells, select the range and view the information on the Status Bar.

To select a range of cells, click on the first cell in the range, and hold down the SHIFT key, then click on the last cell in the range.

Once you have selected the range, look at the lower right-hand side of the Excel **Status Bar**. You will see displayed, the **Average**, **Count**, and **Sum** for the cells you have selected.

	Month 1	Month 2
Jane Smith	$1,000.00	$1,100.00
Peter West	$2,000.00	$1,500.00
Derek Brown	$1,000.00	$1,200.00
Jason Fields	$1,100.00	$1,300.00
Mark Powell	$1,500.00	$1,600.00
Julie Rush	$1,200.00	$1,300.00

eet10 ... ⊕ ⋮ ◀

Average: $1,333.33   Count: 6   Sum: $8,000.00

This provides a way of quickly viewing aggregate data for a range of values in a worksheet without needing to enter the formula(s).

6.6 Calculating Date and Time

Native support for date and time calculations have been vastly improved in Excel over previous editions. You can now carry out many date and time calculations in the worksheet area using arithmetic operators where functions were previously needed. The trick is to apply the right data format to the cells to get the right results. In this section, we will cover some of the most used date and time calculations.

Adding Time

When you enter two numbers separated by a colon sign, for example, 8:45, Excel recognises it as time and will treat it as such when you carry out calculations based on that cell.

Let's say we wanted to calculate how many hours and minutes it took to complete two trips. The first trip took 8 hours and 45 minutes and the second one took 6 hours and 30 minutes.

B5	▼	⋮	×	✓	f_x	=SUM(B3:B4)

◢	A	B	C	D
1				
2		**Time**		
3	Trip 1	08:45		
4	Trip 2	06:30		
5	Total	15:15		
6				

We enter **08:45** in B3 and **06:30** in B4.

The values are added in cell B5 with the formula **=SUM(B3:B4)** and it returns an answer of **15:15** (15 hours and 15 minutes).

As you can see from the example above, when we sum the two values, Excel uses hours and minutes to carry out the calculation rather than hundreds.

Note that Excel only recognises time up to 24 hours by default. If you want to calculate time that is greater than 24 hours, you'll need to format the cell to accept time over 24 hours.

To format the cell, click on the dialog box launcher on the Number group on the Home tab.

In the **Format Cells** dialogue box, click on **Custom**, and in the **Type** field, enter **[h]:mm**. This tells Excel to display values beyond 24 hours.

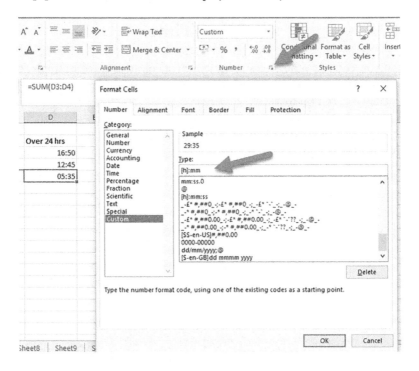

After this change to the cell format, if for example, you add 16:50 + 12:45 you now get 29:35 instead of 05:35.

C4		▼	⋮	×	✓	*fx*	=SUM(C2:C3)	

◢	A	B	C	D
1		Less than 24 hrs	Over 24 hrs	
2	Trip 1	08:45	16:50	
3	Trip 2	06:30	12:45	
4	Total time	15:15	29:35	
5				
6				

Subtracting Time

You can calculate the number of hours between two times by subtracting one from the other, like in a work timesheet, for example.

E4		▼	⋮	×	✓	*fx*	=(D4-B4)-C4

◢	A	B	C	D	E
1	**Timesheet**				
2					
3		Start time	Break (hrs:min)	End time	Total (hrs:min)
4	Mon	9:30 AM	1:00	7:30 PM	9:00
5	Tue	9:00 AM	0:40	5:00 PM	7:20
6	Wed	8:10 AM	0:50	4:30 PM	7:30
7	Thu	7:50 AM	1:30	4:30 PM	7:10
8	Fri	8:00 AM	0:30	4:30 PM	8:00
9					

If you enter the time with a colon between the hours and minutes, a simple subtraction can be used to calculate the difference between two times.

In the example above, the simple formula we need to calculate the total time worked per day is:

=(D4-B4)-C4

This formula first subtracts the **Start time** (B4) from the **End time** (D4), then it subtracts the **Break** (C4) from the difference, to create the total time worked for the day.

Just a few years back, you would need a series of nested IF functions to create the same solution we have achieved above. You would have to carry out all the calculations in hundredths and then use logical tests to derive the minutes. So, Excel (and spreadsheet technology in general) has come a long way since then!

Note: To ensure the elapsed time is displayed correctly, format the cells showing hours and minutes, rather than AM/PM (in this case C4:C8 and E4:E8) with a custom time format - **[h]:mm**. On the other hand, the cells showing AM/PM time (in this case B4:B8 and D4:D8) have been given the custom format - **h:mm AM/PM**.

Calculating Time Across Days

You can use the same method above to calculate the time elapsed across days.

Let's say we have 2 times:

Time 1: *11/24/17 12:30 PM*

Time 2: *11/25/17 2:40 PM*

If Time 1 is in cell **B7** and Time 2 is in cell **C7**, the formula **=C7-B7** will produce the result **26:10** (if the results cell is formatted - **[h]:mm**).

Using the TIME function

You can use the TIME function to properly convert values to hours, minutes and seconds, if directly entered in the formula bar, for example.

Syntax: TIME(hour, minute, second)

Let's say we want to subtract 1 hour 40 minutes from 8:20 AM and we want to just subtract the value in the formula bar rather than enter it in a cell. If the time is in cell A3, we could use the following formula to subtract 1 hour 40 minutes from it:

=A3 - TIME(1,40,0)

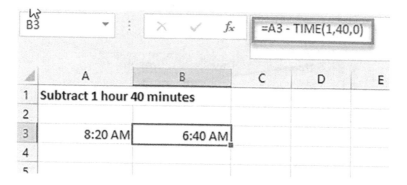

For more on date functions, see chapter 9 - Working with Functions.

Adding and Subtracting Dates

Excel now has improved native functionality for handling dates. For example, in the past, if we wanted to add a number of days to a date, we would need to use a specific function to make the calculation. Now we can just use basic addition and subtraction, and Excel handles all the complexity behind the scenes.

Example 1

Add 40 days to 12/14/2017

1. Enter *12/14/2017* in cell A2 and *40* in cell B2.
2. Enter the formula *=A2+B2* in cell C2
3. Click on Enter.

The result will be *01/23/2018*.

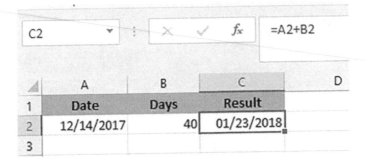

Example 2

Subtract 30 days from 12/14/2017

1. Enter *12/14/2017* in cell A2 and *30* in cell B2.

2. Enter the formula *=A2-B2* in cell C2

3. Click on Enter.

The result will be *11/14/2017*.

| C2 | ▼ | ⋮ | ✕ | ✓ | *fx* | =A2-B2 |

	A	B	C	
1	Date	Days	Result	
2	12/14/2017	30	11/14/2017	
3				

For more on calculating dates, see chapter 9 - **Working with Functions**.

6.7 Relative and Absolute Cell Reference

Relative Cell Reference

By default, a cell reference in Excel is relative. That means, when you refer to cell **B2** from cell **E3**, you are pointing to a cell that is three columns to the left (E minus B), and one row above (3-2). A formula with a relative cell reference changes as you copy it from one cell to another.

For example, if you copy the formula **=C2+D2** from cell E2 to F2, the formula would change to **=D2+E2**. The relative positions of the cells remain one column to the right of the formula.

Examples of relative references:

=D2+E2

=A3*B3

Absolute Cell Reference

If you want to maintain the original cell reference when you copy a formula, you need to make the cell reference *absolute* by inserting a dollar sign (**$**) before the column letter and row number, for example, **=$C$2 + $D$2**. The dollar sign before the column and row tells Excel that the cell reference does not change when the formula is copied to other cells. In this case, when you copy the formula **=$C$2 + $D$2** from E2 to F3, the formula stays the same.

To convert a cell reference to an absolute reference, select the reference in the formula bar (or place the flashing insertion point somewhere in its column letter and row number) and press the **F4** key. For example, if you have =C2 + D2 in the formula bar and you want to make C2 an absolute reference, select C2 in the formula bar and press F4. This will convert it to $C$2.

If you keep pressing F4, Excel will cycle through the different types of cell references available:

- Relative reference (default) - relative columns and rows, for example, A2.

- Absolute reference - absolute columns and rows, for example, $A$2.

- Mixed reference - relative columns and absolute rows, for example, A$2.

- Mixed reference - absolute columns and relative rows, for example, $A2.

Example

In the example below, we're calculating the Sales Tax on various items. The Tax Rate is **20%** and this has been entered in cell B3. The cell format of B3 is *Percentage*.

The formula in cell C6 is **=B6*$B$3**.

As you can see, cell B3 in the formula has been set to an absolute reference. So, when we copy the formula (using autofill) to the rest of the cells under Sales Tax (column C), the reference to cell B3 remains the same.

If the Tax Rate were to change at some point in the future, we would change the value in cell B3 only, and the Sales Tax for all the items will automatically be updated.

| C6 | ▼ | : | × | ✓ | fx | =B6*$B$3 |

▲	A	B	C	D
1	Sales Tax Calculation			
2				
3	Tax Rate:	20%		
4				
5	Product	Price (excl. tax)	Tax	
6	Item 1	$40.00	$8.00	
7	Item 2	$58.00	$11.60	
8	Item 3	$85.00	$17.00	
9	Item 4	$47.00	$9.40	
10	Item 5	$56.00	$11.20	
11	Item 6	$28.00	$5.60	
12	Item 7	$31.00	$6.20	
13	Item 8	$65.00	$13.00	
14	Item 9	$25.90	$5.18	
15	Item 10	$78.30	$15.66	

Mixed Cell Reference

In some cases, you may want to use a "mixed" cell reference. This is where you prefix either the column letter or row number with a dollar sign to lock it in place as an absolute reference, but then allow the other to be a relative reference.

For example, **=$B2 + $C2**

This formula says, the columns part of the cell references (B and C) are locked down as absolute, however, the row (2) is left free to be relative.

When this formula is copied from E4 to F5 (i.e. one column to the right and one row down) it will change to **=$B3 + $C3**. The columns remain the same, however, the row changed because the formula moved one row down. You can also lock down the row and leave the column as relative, for example, **=B$2**.

Examples of mixed references:

=$D2+$E2

=A$3*$B3

6.8 Using Data from Other Worksheets

On some occasions, you may be working on one worksheet and you want to access data on another worksheet in your formula. Or you may decide to separate your summary reports from your data using different worksheets. For example, you may want to have the raw data on **Sheet2** and the summary calculations on **Sheet1**.

Example 1

Let's say we want to create a formula in cell **A6** on **Sheet1** and we want to grab a value from cell **A1** on **Sheet2**.

1. Place the cell pointer in A6 on Sheet1.

2. Enter *=Sheet2!A1* in the formula bar.

3. Click **Enter**.

This will now reference cell A1 from Sheet2 as part of your formula in A6 on Sheet1.

Another way to grab the cell reference is to simply select it with your mouse:

1. Select **A6** on **Sheet1**.
2. Type the equal sign (=) in the formula bar.
3. Click on the **Sheet2** tab (at the bottom of the screen).
4. Select cell **A1** on **Sheet2**.
5. Click **Enter**.

The cell reference *Sheet2!A1* will automatically be entered in A6 on Sheet1. The same method applies for a range. Sometimes you may want your data on one sheet and your summary calculations on another sheet.

If you want to reference more than one cell i.e. a range, you click on Sheet2 and select the range of cells, for example, A1:A10. The reference **Sheet2!A1:A10** will now be added to the formula bar in Sheet1. If you have a named range then you can use the name of the range in place of the cell reference, for example, **Sheet2!MyRange**.

Example 2

In the following example, let's say we have our raw data on Sheet2 and we want to calculate the totals for each Quarter on Sheet1.

B3		:	×	✓	*fx*	=SUM(Sheet2!B2:B13)

◢	A	B	C	D	E
1	Totals for Quarters				
2					
3	QTR1	$6,150.50			
4	QTR2				
5	QTR3				
6	QTR4				
7					
8					

1.   On **Sheet1**, select B3 and in the formula bar, enter *=SUM(.*

2.   Click on **Sheet2**, using the tab at the bottom of the screen.

3.   Select cells **B2:B13** by clicking on B2 and dragging down to B13. This will add *Sheet2!B2:B13* in the formula bar and your syntax should now look like this *=SUM(Sheet2!B2:B13.*

4.   Click in the formula bar and enter the closing bracket. Your formula should now look like this *=SUM(Sheet2!B2:B13).*

5.   Click on **Enter** to confirm the entry.

The sum of the figures from B2 to B13 on Sheet2 will now be shown on sheet1.

7. CREATING DATA VALIDATION RULES

You can insert validation rules in cells to ensure that the data that is entered meets a certain criterion. For example, let's say we want to create a list that will be used by many people. The list has the following columns: *Product Code*, *Product Name*, and *Price*. We want to insert a validation rule to ensure the ***Product Code* is between 5 and 10 characters only**. We could also specify whether we want numbers only, letters only, or a combination of both.

For this example, we will make it a combination of letters and numbers.

Below is an example of how the list would look.

▲	A	B	C
1	Product Code	Product Name	Price
2	NWTB-1	Chai	$18.00
3	NWTCO-3	Syrup	$10.00
4	NWTCO-4	Cajun Seasoning	$22.00
5	NWTO-5	Olive Oil	$21.35
6	NWTJP-6	Boysenberry Spread	$25.00
7	NWTDFN-7	Dried Pears	$30.00
8	NWTS-8	Curry Sauce	$40.00
9	NWTDFN-14	Walnuts	$23.25
10	NWTCFV-17	Fruit Cocktail	$39.00
11	NWTBGM-19	Chocolate Biscuits Mix	$9.20
12	NWTJP-6	Marmalade	$81.00

How to Add a Data Validation Rule

Select the cells for which you want to apply the rule.

Click on the **Data** tab in the ribbon, and in the **Data Tools** group, you will find the **Data Validation** command.

Click on **Data Validation** to launch the Data Validation dialogue box. The box has three tabs, **Settings**, **Input Message**, and **Error Alert**.

On the **Settings** tab, the **Allow** drop-down list gives us several options including, Text length, Whole number, and Decimal. In the **Allow** box, we choose **Text length**.

The **Data** drop-down list provides several comparison operators we can use in our validation criteria. For this example, we want the *Product Code* to be no less than **5** characters and no more than **10** characters.

So, for our validation criteria we'll enter these entries:

- **Allow:** Text length

- **Data:** between

- **Minimum:** 5

- **Maximum:** 10

On the **Input Message** tab, we add a **Title** and the **Input message**. This help message will be displayed as a small pop-up message when the user clicks on a cell with the validation rule.

For this example, we can add a message like:

"The Product Code can be alphanumeric, and it should be between 5 and 10 characters."

In the **Error Alert** tab, we need to enter the message that is displayed when an entry fails the validation rule.

For the **Style,** we have 3 options. **Stop, Warning** and **Information.** We will choose the **Stop** icon for this example as a *Product Code* that does not meet the validation rule cannot be entered.

We can complete the **Title** and **Error Message** with the following:

Title: *"Invalid Entry!"*

Error Message: *"Invalid entry. Please enter a value between 5 and 10 characters in length."*

Data Validation	? ✕
Settings Input Message Error Alert	
☑ Show error alert after invalid data is entered	
When user enters invalid data, show this error alert:	
Style:	Title:
Stop ∨	Invalid Entry!
	Error message:
✕	Invalid entry. Please enter a value between 5 and 10 characters in length
Clear All	OK Cancel

Once you have completed all the tabs, click **OK.**

Data validation will now be applied to the selected cells.

How to Edit or Remove Data Validation Rules

Occasionally you may want to change or remove data validation.

1. Select the cells where data validation has been applied.

2. On the **Data** tab, click on the **Data Validation** command to launch the Data Validation dialogue box.

3. To change the validation rule simply edit the various entries and click OK when done.

4. To remove the validation rule, click **Clear All**.

5. Click **OK**.

8. NAMED RANGES

When working with a lot of data, it is sometimes useful to identify your data as a group with one name to make it easier to reference in your formulas. A Named Range is a group of cells in Excel that have been selected and given one name. After you give the selection a name, the whole range can now be referenced as one unit using that name in Excel formulas and functions. This is like a table with a name.

For example, we may have a list of contacts we would like to use in formulas. We could either use A1:G17 to identify the range of data or name the range "Contacts" and then use that name to reference the data from then on.

	A	B	C	D	E	F	G
1	Company	Last Name	First Name	Job Title	Address	City	State/Province
2	Company A	Bedecs	Anna	Owner	123 1st Street	Seattle	WA
3	Company B	Gratacos Solsona	Antonio	Owner	123 2nd Street	Boston	MA
4	Company C	Axen	Thomas	Purchasing Representative	123 3rd Street	Los Angelas	CA
5	Company D	Lee	Christina	Purchasing Manager	123 4th Street	New York	NY
6	Company E	O'Donnell	Martin	Owner	123 5th Street	Minneapolis	MN
7	Company F	Pérez-Olaeta	Francisco	Purchasing Manager	123 6th Street	Milwaukee	WI
8	Company G	Xie	Ming-Yang	Owner	123 7th Street	Boise	ID
9	Company H	Andersen	Elizabeth	Purchasing Representative	123 8th Street	Portland	OR
10	Company I	Mortensen	Sven	Purchasing Manager	123 9th Street	Salt Lake City	UT
11	Company J	Wacker	Roland	Purchasing Manager	123 10th Street	Chicago	IL
12	Company K	Krschne	Peter	Purchasing Manager	123 11th Street	Miami	FL
13	Company L	Edwards	John	Purchasing Manager	123 12th Street	Las Vegas	NV
14	Company M	Ludick	Andre	Purchasing Representative	456 13th Street	Memphis	TN
15	Company N	Grilo	Carlos	Purchasing Representative	456 14th Street	Denver	CO
16	Company O	Kupkova	Helena	Purchasing Manager	456 15th Street	Honolulu	HI
17	Company P	Goldschmidt	Daniel	Purchasing Representative	456 16th Street	San Francisco	CA

One of the benefits of using a named range is that the name is an absolute reference. When you create a formula with that name, you can copy and paste the formula in any part of your workbook, including different worksheets in the workbook, and the name will always point to the same group of cells.

8.1 Creating a Named Range

There are two ways you can create a named range:

Method 1

1. Select the cells you want to include in the named range.

2. Click in the Name box (this is the box on the left side of the screen, just above the worksheet area) and enter the name for your named range.

3. Press **Enter** on your keyboard to save the name.

In the example below, I selected A1:G17 and entered "Contacts" in the name box to name that range. I can now use Contacts in place of A1:G17 in all formulas and functions in this workbook.

By default, when you create a Named Range it will be available across all worksheets in that workbook.

Contacts ▼			✕ ✓ f_x	Company			
	A	B	C	D	E	F	G
1	Company	Last Name	First Name	Job Title	Address	City	State/Province
2	Company A	Bedecs	Anna	Owner	123 1st Street	Seattle	WA
3	Company B	Gratacos Solsona	Antonio	Owner	123 2nd Street	Boston	MA
4	Company C	Axen	Thomas	Purchasing Representative	123 3rd Street	Los Angelas	CA
5	Company D	Lee	Christina	Purchasing Manager	123 4th Street	New York	NY
6	Company E	O'Donnell	Martin	Owner	123 5th Street	Minneapolis	MN
7	Company F	Pérez-Olaeta	Francisco	Purchasing Manager	123 6th Street	Milwaukee	WI
8	Company G	Xie	Ming-Yang	Owner	123 7th Street	Boise	ID
9	Company H	Andersen	Elizabeth	Purchasing Representative	123 8th Street	Portland	OR
10	Company I	Mortensen	Sven	Purchasing Manager	123 9th Street	Salt Lake City	UT
11	Company J	Wacker	Roland	Purchasing Manager	123 10th Street	Chicago	IL
12	Company K	Krschne	Peter	Purchasing Manager	123 11th Street	Miami	FL
13	Company L	Edwards	John	Purchasing Manager	123 12th Street	Las Vegas	NV
14	Company M	Ludick	Andre	Purchasing Representative	456 13th Street	Memphis	TN
15	Company N	Grilo	Carlos	Purchasing Representative	456 14th Street	Denver	CO
16	Company O	Kupkova	Helena	Purchasing Manager	456 15th Street	Honolulu	HI
17	Company P	Goldschmidt	Daniel	Purchasing Representative	456 16th Street	San Francisco	CA

Method 2

1. Select the cells you want to include in the named range.

2. Click on the Formulas tab on the ribbon. On the **Defined Names** group, click on **Define Name**.

3. A dialogue box will be displayed that allows you to enter the name. Leave the Scope field as Workbook (which is the default) if you wish to reference the name in different worksheets in the workbook. You can also use the up-arrow next to the **Refers to** field to reselect the range.

4. Click **OK** when done.

8.2 Editing a Named Range

1. On the Formulas tab, click **Name Manager** (in the Defined Names group).

2. The Name Manager dialogue box will be displayed with a list of all the named ranges and tables in the workbook.

3. On the list, select the named range you want to edit and click on the **Edit...** button.

Name Manager				?	×
New...	Edit...	Delete			Filter ▾
Name	Value	Refers To	Scope	Comment	
Customers	{"Company A","Bedec...	=Sheet3!$A$2:$H$30	Workbo...		
Holidays_range	{...}	='C:\Users\George\...	Workbo...		
Scores	{"44","69","25","83","3...	=Sheet1!$B$2:$G$21	Workbo...		
Table1	{"230923100","2309-2...	='Number Format'!...	Workbo...		
Table5	{"Andersen","Elizabet...	='Sample Data'!$A...	Workbo...		
TestRange	{"Chai","$1,800.00";"B...	=Charts!$A$2:$B$16	Workbo...		

Refers to:
=Sheet3!$A$2:$H$30

Close

4. On the next screen, you can change the name of the range in the **Name** field.

5. To change the area that makes up the range, click in the **Refers to** field. A scrolling marquee will appear around the current range. You can now select a new area or hold down the **Shift** key and adjust the current selection with your mouse pointer.

6. Click **OK** on the Edit Name box.

7. Click **Close**.

8.3 Deleting a Named Range

1. On the **Formulas** tab, click **Name Manager**.

2. Select the named range you want to delete from the list.

3. Click the **Delete** button.

4. Click **Close** when done.

8.4 How to Use a Named Range

To select a named range, click the dropdown arrow of the name box and select the name from the drop-down list. This will display the worksheet with the range (if you're on a different worksheet) and select all the rows and columns in the range.

A1		⋮	×	✓	*fx*	Orders
Customers						
Orders_Range			B			C
Scores						
TestRange						
Table1			Customer			Order Date
Table5			Henderson			1/15/2019
			Anderson			2/2/2019
5			Earl Foster			3/3/2019
6			Sean Hill			4/4/2019
7						

Example

The following example demonstrates the use of a named range called *Orders_Range* in place of the cell reference A1:D13. The example uses two formulas to count numeric values and blank cells in the range. The name of the range has been used as arguments in the functions instead of A1:D13.

=COUNT(Orders_Range)

=COUNTBLANK(Orders_Range)

Orders_Range	▾	⋮	×	✓	*fx*	Orders	
	A	B	C	D			E
1	**Orders**						
2		**Customer**	**Order Date**	**Order Total**			
3	Sector 1	Bruce Henderson	1/15/2019	$2,635			
4		Louis Anderson	2/2/2019	$7,227			
5		Earl Foster	3/3/2019	$4,426			
6		Sean Hill	4/4/2019	$8,774			
7							
8	Sector 2	Benjamin Martinez	4/12/2019	$9,829			
9		Joe Perez	4/15/2019	$2,194			
10		Shawn Johnson	4/17/2019	$2,459			
11		Kenneth Roberts	5/8/2019	$3,920			
12		Cynthia Martin	5/19/2019	$2,566			
13		Susan Mitchell	6/10/2019	$7,034			
14							
15			Numeric values		20 =COUNT(Orders_Range)		
16			Blank cells		16 =COUNTBLANK(Orders_Range)		
17							
18							

9. WORKING WITH FUNCTIONS

The Excel function library is vast, ranging from basic aggregate functions to more specialized functions for statisticians, mathematicians and engineers. In this book, we will be covering some of the most useful functions for everyday Excel tasks at home or at work.

The more specialized and dedicated functions are outside the scope of this book. However, information is provided at the end of the chapter for how to access other functions in Excel.

In this chapter we will cover:

- Aggregate functions that enable you to calculate the sum, average, min, max, and count.

- The IF function that enables you to carry out evaluations based on logical tests.

- The VLOOKUP function that enables you to find and return a value in a list, table, or range based on a lookup value.

- Date functions that enable you to calculate the difference between two dates.

- Functions that enable you to add or subtract days, months, or years to/from any given date.

- Text functions that enable you to manipulate and rearrange text strings.

9.1 How to Enter a Function

You enter a function in the same way you enter a formula. All functions have an opening and closing bracket and most functions have arguments enclosed in the brackets.

A **function argument** is a piece of data that a function needs in order to run. Most functions need at least one argument but a select few, like the *Today()* and *Now()* functions do not have arguments.

To insert a function:

1. Click in the cell where you want to display the result.

2. Click in the formula bar.

3. Enter an equal sign (=) and start typing the function name. At this point you'll get a dropdown list with all the Excel functions related to your entry.

4. Use your up/down arrow keys to highlight the function you want on the list and press the **Tab** key once to select it. This will enter the function and the opening bracket in the formula bar, enabling you to enter the argument(s).

5. Enter the argument(s) and the closing bracket, for example, =SUM(C1:C4).

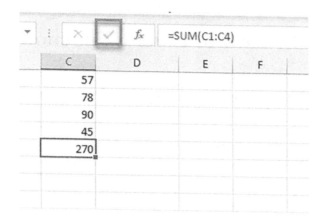

6. Click on **Enter** or press the **Enter** key to confirm your entry.

Tip: As much as possible, avoid typing cell references directly into the formula bar as it could introduce errors. Instead, enter the name of the formula and the open bracket, for example, enter =SUM(. Then select the cells you want for your argument in the worksheet itself before entering the closing bracket.

Using the Insert Function Dialogue Box

A second way you can enter a function is by using the **Insert Function** dialogue box.

Click in the formula bar to place the cursor there and click the **Insert Function** command on the **Formulas** tab, or the Insert Function button next to the formula bar.

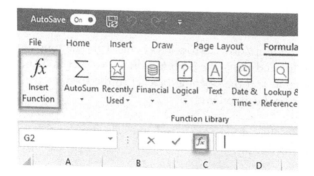

This will display the **Insert Function** dialogue box. This dialogue box provides the option to search for the function or select it from a category.

To search for the function, enter the name of the function in the **Search for a function** box. For example, if you were searching for the IF function you would enter IF in the search box and click **Go**. The **Select a function** list will display all the functions related to your search term.

You can also use the **category** drop-down list to select a function if you know its category in Excel. For example, you can find the IF function in the **Logical** category.

If you have used a function recently it'll be listed in the **Most Recently Used** category.

When you select a function on the list, you'll see the syntax for the function and a description of what the function does below the list.

Once you've selected the one you want, click **OK** to go to the **Functions Arguments** window.

The Functions Arguments window enables you to enter the arguments for the function. This dialogue box is particularly useful if you are not familiar with a function because it provides a description of each argument, a preview of your entries, and the result returned by the function.

f_x | =IF(A4 >100,"Over Budget","Within Budget")

D	E	F	G	H	I	J	K	L	M

Function Arguments   ?   ✕

IF

Logical_test	A4 > 100	⬆	= FALSE
Value_if_true	"Over Budget"	⬆	= "Over Budget"
Value_if_false	"Within Budget"	⬆	= "Within Budget"

= "Within Budget"

Checks whether a condition is met, and returns one value if TRUE, and another value if FALSE.

Value_if_false is the value that is returned if Logical_test is FALSE. If omitted, FALSE is returned.

Formula result = Within Budget

Help on this function   OK   Cancel

After entering the arguments, click **OK** and the formula will be inserted in the formula bar.

9.2 Aggregate Functions

An aggregate function is a function that groups values from multiple rows into a single value. This provides a summary that adds meaning to the data, depending on what we're analysing. Aggregate functions include SUM, AVERAGE, MIN, MAX etc.

SUM Function

The SUM function enables you to add values on your spreadsheet. You can add individual values, cell references, ranges or a mix of all three. You can sum up contiguous cells or non-contiguous cells.

Syntax

SUM(number1,[number2],...)

Arguments

Argument	Description
Number1	Required. The first cell reference, range, or number for which you want to calculate the sum. The argument can be a number like 4, a cell reference like A10, or a range like A2:A10.
Number2, ...	Optional. Additional cell references, ranges or numbers for which you want to calculate the sum, up to a maximum of 255.

Example 1 - Summing contiguous data:

In this example, we have values in cells B2 to B13 that you want to sum up. We could either use the AutoSum command on the ribbon or enter the formula in the formula bar:

=SUM(B2:B13)

Entering the formula manually:

1. Select the cell you want to use for the sum. In this case, it is B14.

2. Click in the formula bar and enter **=SUM(**.

3. Select B2 and drag down to B13.

4. Type **)** in the formula bar to close the function.

    The contents of the formula bar should now look like this **=SUM(B2:B13)**.

5. Click the **Enter** button or press **Enter** on your keyboard.

| SUM | ▼ | ⁝ | ✕ ✓ *fx* | =SUM(B2:B13) |

◢	A	B	C	D	E
1	**Month**	**Expenses**			
2	Jan	$400.00			
3	Feb	$640.00			
4	Mar	$550.00			
5	Apr	$420.00			
6	May	$310.50			
7	Jun	$566.30			
8	Jul	$607.90			
9	Aug	$300.80			
10	Sep	$500.50			
11	Oct	$700.00			
12	Nov	$840.00			
13	Dec	$900.00			
14	Sum	=SUM(B2:B13)			
15		SUM(**number1**, [number2], ...)			
16					

Example 2: Summing non-contiguous data:

To sum up data in different ranges, i.e. non-contiguous data, you can enter the ranges as different arguments in the SUM function.

For example:

=SUM(B2:B13,D2:D13,F2:F13,H2:H13)

Entering the formula:

1. Select the cell where you want to place the formula.

2. Click in the formula bar and type in the function name with the opening bracket. For example *=SUM(.*

3. Select the first range.

4. Type in a comma i.e. *=SUM(B2:B13,.*

5. Select the next range and type in a comma.

6. Select any additional ranges, making sure you type a comma after each range.

7. Type in the closing bracket. You should now have something like this: *=SUM(B2:B13,D2:D13,F2:F13,H2:H13).*

8. Click **Enter** to confirm your entry.

H2	▾	:	✕	✓	*fx*	=SUM(B2:B13,D2:D13,F2:F13,H2:H13)

	A	B	C	D	E	F	G	H	I
1	**Month**	**QTR1**		**QTR2**		**QTR3**		**QTR4**	
2	Jan	$420.00		$566.30		$400.00		$840.00	
3	Feb	$210.00		$640.00		$607.90		$340.00	
4	Mar	$340.00		$550.00		$600.00		$607.90	
5	Apr	$420.00		$607.90		$400.00		$420.00	
6	May	$310.50		$500.00		$210.00		$400.00	
7	Jun	$500.00		$566.30		$420.00		$607.90	
8	Jul	$300.00		$607.90		$505.00		$790.00	
9	Aug	$700.00		$400.00		$500.00		$733.00	
10	Sep	$410.00		$500.50		$900.00		$500.50	
11	Oct	$800.00		$607.90		$700.00		$600.00	
12	Nov	$840.00		$840.00		$840.00		$300.00	
13	Dec	$900.00		$1,100.00		$1,200.00		$1,000.00	
14									
15	**Total**							3,H2:H13)	

AVERAGE Function

The AVERAGE function is one of the widely used aggregate functions in Excel. It returns the average of the arguments. The average is the arithmetic mean of a series of numbers and is calculated by adding up the numbers and then dividing by the count of those numbers.

Syntax

AVERAGE(number1, [number2], ...)

Arguments

Argument	Description
Number1	Required. The first cell reference, range or number for which you want to calculate an average.
Number2, ...	Optional. Additional cell references, ranges or numbers for which you want to calculate an average, up to a maximum of 255.

Notes

- Arguments can be numbers, named ranges, or cell references that contain numbers.

- If any of the cells referenced in the arguments contain an error value, AVERAGE returns an error.

- Text, logical values, and empty cells are ignored, however, cells with the value zero (0) are included.

Example

In the example below, we use the AVERAGE function to calculate the average of the scores in range B2:C16.

Formula: =AVERAGE(B2:C16)

F1			×	✓	fx	=AVERAGE(B2:C16)	

⊿	A	B	C	D	E	F
1	Student	Subject 1	Subject 2		Average score	53.3
2	Bruce	0	55			
3	Louis	57	61			
4	Earl	51	47			
5	Sean	74	74			
6	Benjamin	50	50			
7	Joe	30	52			
8	Shawn	95	N/A			
9	Kenneth	8	70			
10	Cynthia	30	45			
11	Susan	57	40			
12	John	67	76			
13	Bruce	81	60			
14	Louis	50	61			
15	Earl	30	47			
16	Kenneth	79	50			

Notice that one of the cells has N/A. That cell will be ignored and not counted as part of the average.

MAX, MIN, MEDIAN Functions

The MAX, MIN and MEDIAN functions are some of the most commonly used functions in Excel and are very similar in their arguments and how they're used. MAX returns the largest number in a specified set of values. MIN returns the smallest number in a set of values. MEDIAN returns the median which is the number in the middle of a set of numbers.

Syntax

Max function: MAX(number1, [number2], ...)

Min function: MIN(number1, [number2], ...)

Median function: MEDIAN(number1, [number2], ...)

Arguments – similar for all three functions

Argument	Description
Number1	Required. The first argument is required and can be a number, range, array, or reference that contain numbers.
number2, ...	Optional. You can have additional numbers, cell references, or ranges up to a maximum of 255 arguments which you want to evaluate.

Remarks

- The functions will return 0 (zero) if the arguments contain no numbers.

- If an argument is a reference or an array, only numbers in that reference or array are used. Logical values, text values, empty cells in the reference or array are ignored.

- The functions will return an error if arguments contain error values or text that cannot be translated into numbers.

- Text representations of numbers and logical values that you directly type into the arguments list are counted.

- For the MEDIAN function, if there is an even number of numeric values in the set, it calculates the average of the two numbers in the middle.

Example

In the example below, we want to show the maximum, minimum, and median values for the Sales column (D2:D12) in our table.

The following formulas return the desired results:

- MAX(D2:D12)

- MIN(D2:D12)

- MEDIAN(D2:D12)

G2			fx	=MAX(D2:D12)			
	A	B	C	D	E	F	G	H
1	Name	State	No. Orders	Sales		Report		
2	Bruce	New York	51	$74,298		Highest sales	$95,778	=MAX(D2:D12)
3	Louis	New York	39	$46,039		Lowest sales	$33,340	=MIN(D2:D12)
4	Earl	Washington	60	$65,252		Median	$58,808	=MEDIAN(D2:D12)
5	Sean	Washington	100	$61,847				
6	Benjamin	Texas	28	$33,340				
7	Joe	California	31	$95,778				
8	Shawn	Texas	35	$58,808				
9	Kenneth	California	39	$52,593				
10	Cynthia	California	51	$42,484				
11	Susan	Texas	80	$44,390				
12	Dav	New York	70	$66,109				
13								

To add more cell references or ranges to the arguments you simply separate them with a comma, for example, MAX(C1:C5, G1:G5).

COUNT Function

The COUNT function will count the number of cells that contain numbers in a range, or a list of numbers provided as arguments. The COUNT function only counts populated cells. For example, if you have a range with 20 cells, and only 5 of the cells have numbers, the count function will return 5.

Syntax

COUNT(value1, [value2], ...)

Arguments

Argument	Description
Value1	Required. The first range within which you want to count numbers.
Value2	Optional. Additional cell references or ranges in which you want to count numbers. You can have a maximum of 255 arguments for this function.

Remarks

- You can have a maximum of 255 arguments for this function. Each argument could be a number, a cell reference, or a range.

- The COUNT function counts numbers, dates, or text representations of numbers (i.e. a number enclosed in quotation marks, like "1").

- Error values or text that cannot be translated into numbers are not counted.

- Use the COUNTIF function or the COUNTIFS function if you want to count only numbers that meet a specific condition.

Example

In this example, we use the COUNT function to count the values in two ranges.

The formula is:

=COUNT(A3:D20,F3:I20)

L2 =COUNT(A3:D20,F3:I20)

| | 2018 | | | | | 2019 | | | | | Count | 131 |
A (QTR1)	B (QTR2)	C (QTR3)	D (QTR4)	E	F (QTR1)	G (QTR2)	H (QTR3)	I (QTR4)	J	K	L	
70	83	16	37		26	56	47	17				
73	71	88	52		87	57	36	87				
38	65		19		38	50	51	68				
87	56	91	55		62	40	26	77				
18	97	39	82			98	98	25				
86	15		85		47	59	60	61				
28		98	86		41	19	10	11				
45	80	43	73			92	95	59				
60	92	98	34		51	38	13	91				
51	64	25	50		81	84		60				
79	29	69	27		62	69	17	65				
65	54	95	22		73	53	40	67				
91		10	91		66		83	74				
88	97	91	89		48	58	78	25				
40	88		15		66	12	55	85				
12	54	22	87		59	10	66	20				
42	17	51	33				67	26				
78			32		52	32	62	61				

This is a simple formula with two arguments to represent the two ranges in which we want to count values: A3:D20 and F3:I20. Note that the blank cells are not counted.

9.3 Conditional Functions

A conditional function requires a test before carrying out one of two calculations. If the test evaluates to TRUE it executes one statement, and if the test is FALSE, it executes a different statement. The statements can be calculations, text, or even other functions.

A conditional function requires:
1. The logical test to carry out.
2. What to return if the test is TRUE.
3. What to return if the test is FALSE.

Conditional functions can also be nested if we have more than one test to carry out.

IF Function

The IF function is one of the popular functions in Excel used to create conditional formulas. The IF function allows you to carry out a logical test (using comparison operators) that evaluates to TRUE or FALSE. It then returns one value if TRUE and another if FALSE.

Syntax:

IF(logical_test, value_if_true, [value_if_false])

Arguments

Argument	Description
logical_test	Required. This is a value or expression that can be evaluated to TRUE or FALSE.
value_if_true	Required. This is the value that's returned if the logical test is true.
value_if_false	Optional. This is the value that's returned if the logical test is false. If the logical test is FALSE and this argument is omitted, nothing happens.

In its simplest form this is what the function says:

IF (something is TRUE, then do A, otherwise do B)

Therefore, the IF function will return a different result for TRUE and FALSE.

Entering IF with Insert Function

If you're new to the IF function, you might want to use the **Insert Function** dialogue box to enter the function. This process provides a wizard that guides you through entering the function arguments, enabling you to see if your logical test is producing the result you want. The **Function Arguments** window enables you to debug your logical tests and fix any errors before you insert the function.

See chapter 9.1 – **How to Enter a Function**, for how to use the Insert Function process.

Example 1

A simple way the IF function is commonly used is to determine if a calculated cell has any value or not. If the result is 0 then it returns a blank cell.

In the example below, the formula for the total for *Jan* was entered in cell **I2** and we want to drag the formula down to populate the totals for *Feb* to *Dec*. Without the IF function, it would display $0 for the unpopulated months, however, we want the totals for the unpopulated months to be blank instead of $0 even with the formula in place.

Thus, the formula for Jan in cell **I2** is:

=IF(SUM(B2:H2) >0,SUM(B2:H2) ,"")

The IF function in this example checks to see if the sum of Jan is greater than zero. If true it returns the sum. If it is false, then it returns a blank string.

When we populate the other fields with the formula, we get the following.

2			f_x	=IF(SUM(B2:H2) > 0,SUM(B2:H2),"")					

	A	B	C	D	E	F	G	H	I	J
	Month	QTR1		QTR2		QTR3		QTR4	Total for Year	
	Jan	$420.00		$566.30		$400.00		$840.00	2226.3	
	Feb	$210.00		$640.00		$607.90		$340.00	1797.9	
	Mar	$340.00		$550.00		$600.00		$607.90	2097.9	
	Apr	$420.00		$607.90		$400.00		$420.00	1847.9	
	May									
	Jun									
	Jul									
	Aug									
	Sep									
	Oct									
	Nov									
	Dec									

Example 2

In another example, we could use the results of an evaluation to return different values in our worksheet.

Let's say we have a budgeting sheet and want to use a "Status" column to report on how the **Actual** figure compares to the **Budgeted** figure. In this case, we can use the IF statement to test whether the actual figure is greater than the budgeted figure. If **Actual** is greater than **Budgeted**, the formula would enter "Over Budget", otherwise it would enter "Within Budget".

C2			f_x	=IF(B2 > A2,"Over Budget", "Within Budget")					

	A	B	C	D	E	F	G
1	Budgeted	Actual	Status				
2	$1,000.00	$900.00	Within Budget				
3	$2,000.00	$1,100.00	Within Budget				
4	$2,500.00	$1,500.00	Within Budget				
5	$2,300.00	$2,100.00	Within Budget				
6	$1,500.00	$2,300.00	Over Budget				
7	$1,200.00	$2,100.00	Over Budget				
8	$2,050.00	$2,030.00	Within Budget				
9	$5,000.00	$4,100.00	Within Budget				
10	$3,000.00	$2,100.00	Within Budget				
11							

=IF(B2 > A2,"Over Budget", "Within Budget")

The IF function checks to see if the value in B2 is greater than the value in A2. If it is, it returns "Over Budget" otherwise it returns "Within Budget".

Example 3

In another example, say we have products for sale and when **10 or more** of a product is purchased we apply a **10%** promotional discount.

The logical test checks if C4 is greater than or equal to 10.

If true it returns the subtotal minus 10%.

If false it returns the subtotal.

=IF(C4>=10,D4 - (D4 * 0.1),D4)

When we populate the other cells with the AutoFill handle (a + sign that appears when you place the mouse pointer on the lower-right corner of the active cell) we get the following result.

E4				fx	=IF(C4>=10,D4 - (D4 * 0.1),D4)		
	A	B	C	D	E		F
1	Sales						
2							
3	Product	Cost	Quantity	Sub-Total	Total (with discount)	Formulatext	
4	Beer	$1.50	15	$22.50	$20.25	=IF(C4>=10,D4 - (D4 * 0.1),D4)	
5	Brownie Mix	$4.20	10	$42.00	$37.80	=IF(C5>=10,D5 - (D5 * 0.1),D5)	
6	Cake Mix	$4.80	10	$48.00	$43.20	=IF(C6>=10,D6 - (D6 * 0.1),D6)	
7	Chai	$1.80	10	$18.00	$16.20	=IF(C7>=10,D7 - (D7 * 0.1),D7)	
8	Chocolate Biscuits Mix	$5.20	5	$26.00	$26.00	=IF(C8>=10,D8 - (D8 * 0.1),D8)	
9	Coffee	$2.00	25	$50.00	$45.00	=IF(C9>=10,D9 - (D9 * 0.1),D9)	
10	Green Tea	$2.00	50	$100.00	$90.00	=IF(C10>=10,D10 - (D10 * 0.1),D10)	
11	Scones	$4.90	5	$24.50	$24.50	=IF(C11>=10,D11 - (D11 * 0.1),D11)	
12	Tea	$1.30	20	$26.00	$23.40	=IF(C12>=10,D12 - (D12 * 0.1),D12)	
13							
14							
15	*Apply a 10% discount if the quantity sold per item is 10 or more.						

Nested IF Functions

on as an argument within another IF function. This

nent.

A nested IF function might be required if you need to carry out more than one logical test in your function. In the example below, we use a nested IF statement to test for 3 possible values and return a different result for each one.

Let's say we have a spreadsheet to record the score of exams and we want to mark everything under 40 as FAIL, between 40 and 69 as CREDIT, and 70 or more as MERIT.

The formula would look like this:

=IF(A2 < 40, "FAIL",IF(A2 < 70,"CREDIT","MERIT"))

B2	▼	:	×	✓	f_x	=IF(A2 < 40, "FAIL",IF(A2 < 70,"CREDIT","MERIT"))		
	A	B	C	D	E	F	G
1	Score	Result					
2	70	MERIT					
3							

Formula explanation:

The first IF function checks if A2 is less than 40. If it is true it returns FAIL. If it is false, it executes the second IF function.

The second IF function checks if A2 is less than 70. If true it returns CREDIT, and if false, it returns MERIT.

Advanced IF Functions

Excel 2019 also includes several other conditional functions you could use in place of the standard IF function. These functions are a combination of a logical function and an aggregate function. These are known as advanced IF functions, hence outside the scope of this book regarding in-depth coverage.

To learn more about these functions, enter the function name in the **Tell Me** box on the Excel ribbon and choose *Get Help for [function name]* from the pop up menu.

Also, for an in-depth coverage of these advanced functions, you could check out my book *Excel 2019 Functions* which is a guide for Excel functions that goes beyond the basics.

AVERAGEIF

Syntax:

=AVERAGEIF(range, criteria, [average_range])

This function returns the average (arithmetic mean) of data that meets the value you've entered as your criteria. The optional *average_range* argument allows you to specify another range for the values if it is separate from the one with the criteria.

Example:

=AVERAGEIF(A2:A20,"<2000")

This means return the average of all the values in cells A2 to A20 that are over 2000.

AVERAGEIFS

Syntax:

=AVERAGEIFS(average_range, criteria_range1, criteria1, [criteria_range2, criteria2], ...)

This function is similar to AVERAGEIF, however, it allows you to specify multiple ranges and multiple criteria in the arguments. You can specify up to 127 ranges and criteria.

COUNTIF

This function returns the count of the values in a range that meets the specified criteria.

Syntax:

=COUNTIF(range, criteria)

In its simplest form this function says:

=COUNTIF(Where do you want to look?, What do you want to look for?)

Example:

=COUNTIF(A2:A10,"New York")

This will return the count of the number of cells in A2:A10 with the value "New York".

COUNTIFS

COUNTIFS(criteria_range1, criteria1, [criteria_range2, criteria2]…)

This function is like the COUNTIF function in that it returns a count based on a condition you specify. However, you can specify multiple ranges and criteria. You can specify up to 127 range/criteria pairs.

SUMIF

This function returns the sum of values in a range that match a given criterion.

Example:

=SUMIF(A2:A10, ">10")

This means return the sum of all the values in cells A2 to A10 that are greater than 10.

SUMIFS

Syntax:

SUMIFS(sum_range, criteria_range1, criteria1, [criteria_range2, criteria2], ...)

This function returns the sum of values that meet multiple criteria. You can specify up to 127 range/criteria pairs.

9.4 Date Functions

Date functions enable you to calculate and manipulate date and time. In this section, we will be covering the most common date functions for general use.

Note that you can now carry out some date calculations in Excel without the use of functions. Some date and time calculations that required a function in the past can now be done natively in Excel using arithmetic operators. See the section in this book on Calculating Date and Time for more. The date convention that has been used in the following examples is MM/DD/YYYY.

Note: Excel sometimes automatically detects a date entry and formats the cell accordingly. However, if you copied and pasted a date from another source, you may need to manually format the cell to a date to display the date properly.

DATE Function

The DATE function enables you to combine different values into a single date.

Syntax

DATE (year, month, day)

Arguments

Argument	Description
Year	Required. This argument can have one to four digits. Excel uses the date system on your computer to interpret the year argument.

Month	Required. The month argument should be a positive or negative integer between 1 to 12, representing January to December. If the month argument is a negative number (-*n*) the function returns a date that is *n* months back from the last month of the previous year. For example, DATE(2019,-4,2) will return the serial number representing August 2, 2018.
Day	Required. This argument can be a positive or negative integer from 1 to 31, representing the day of the month.

If the month argument is greater than 12, the function adds that number of months to the last month of the specified year. If Day is greater than the number of days in the specified month, the function adds that number of days to the first day of the next month of the specified date.

Tip: To prevent unwanted results, always use four digits for the year argument. For example, "04" could mean "1904" or "2004." Using four-digit years prevents any confusion.

Example 1

In this example, we want to combine values from different cells for the month, day, and year into a date value recognised in Excel.

- Month: 4
- Day: 14
- Year: 2018

When we use the DATE function to combine the values into a single date, we get the following:

=DATE(C2,A2,B2)

	A	B	C	D	E
1	Month	Day	Year	Combined Date	
2	4		14	2018	4/14/2018
3					

D2 — fx =DATE(C2,A2,B2)

Example 2

To calculate the date, we combine the YEAR, MONTH, and DAY functions with the DATE function.

- YEAR returns the year corresponding to a date entered as its argument.

- MONTH returns the month corresponding to a date entered as its argument.

- DAY returns the day corresponding to a date entered as its argument.

When we combine these functions with the DATE function, we get the following formula:

=DATE(YEAR(A3)+B3,MONTH(A3),DAY(A3))

Answer: 12/15/2023.

C3 — fx =DATE(YEAR(A3)+B3,MONTH(A3),DAY(A3))

	A	B	C	D	E	F	G
1	Contracts						
2	Start Date	Duration	End Date				
3	12/15/2017	6	12/15/2023				

Formula Explanation

=DATE(YEAR(A3)+B3,MONTH(A3),DAY(A3))

The *year* argument of the DATE function has **YEAR(A3)+B3**. This will return 2023 (i.e. 2017 + 6). The other functions return the month and day respectively in the *month* and *day* arguments.

To subtract years, use the minus sign (–) in place of the plus sign (+) in the formula.

Example 3

In this example, we want to add 15 months to December 15, 2017.

Formula:

=DATE(YEAR(A3),MONTH(A3)+B3,DAY(A3))

Answer: 03/15/2019

C3			×	✓	*fx*	=DATE(YEAR(A3),MONTH(A3)+B3,DAY(A3))			

◢	A	B	C	D	E	F	G
1	Contracts						
2	**Start Date**	**Months**	**End Date**				
3	12/15/2017	15	03/15/2019				
4							

Formula Explanation

In the *month* argument of the DATE function, the syntax, **MONTH(A3)+B3** is what is used to add 15 months to the date. The DATE function will automatically calculate the date from the arguments provided.

To subtract months, use the – sign in place of the + sign in the formula.

Example 4

In this example, we want to add 20 days to December 15, 2017.

Formula:

=DATE(YEAR(A3),MONTH(A3),DAY(A3)+B3)

Answer: 1/4/2018

C3			✗	✓	fx	=DATE(YEAR(A3),MONTH(A3),DAY(A3)+B3)			
	A	B		C		D	E	F	G
1	Contracts								
2	Start Date	Days		End Date					
3	12/15/2017	20		01/04/2018					
4									

Formula Explanation

The 20 days were added to the DAY function in the *day* argument (i.e. DAY(A3)+B3) of the DATE function. The DATE function accurately returns the End Date based on the input we've provided.

To subtract days, use the minus sign (–) in place of the plus sign (+) in the formula.

To find the difference between two dates you can use the DATEDIF which is covered later in this chapter.

DATEDIF Function

The DATEDIF function calculates the difference between two dates. This function provides one of the easiest ways in Excel to calculate the difference between two dates. It can return the number of days, months, or years between two dates.

DATEDIF is a "hidden" function in Excel because you'll not find it on the list of date functions or when you search for it using the Insert Function dialogue box. You must enter it manually any time you want to use it. It is a legacy function from Lotus 1-2-3 but operational on all versions of Excel.

Syntax

DATEDIF(start_date, end_date, unit)

Arguments

Argument	Description
start_date	Required. This argument represents the start date of the period.
end_date	Required. This argument represents the end date of the period.
unit	Required. This argument represents the unit of measurement you want to return - days, months, or years. It should be entered as a string.
	It can be one of Y, M, D, YM, or YD.
	"Y" = Calculates the number of years in the period.
	"M" = Calculates the number of months in the period.
	"D" = Calculates the number of days in the period.
	"YM" = Calculates the difference between the months in start_date and end_date. The days and years of the dates are ignored.
	"YD" = Calculates the difference between the days of start_date and end_date. The years of the dates are ignored.

Note: There is also an "MD" argument that calculates the number of days while ignoring the month and years. However, Microsoft no longer recommends the use of the MD argument in this function because under some conditions it could return a negative number.

Example 1

In the example below, we want to calculate the age of someone born on December 1, 1980.

Formula:

=DATEDIF(A2,TODAY(),"Y")

B2	▼	⋮	⤬	✓	*fx*	=DATEDIF(A2,TODAY(),"Y")		
◢	A	B	C	D	E	F		
1	Date of Birth	Years						
2	12/1/1980	38						
3								

We combined the DATEDIF function with the TODAY function to get the desired result. The TODAY function returns today's date, so this formula will always use today's date to calculate the age. The "Y" argument returns the difference in years.

Example 2

To calculate the number of months between two dates we use the "M" argument of the function.

=DATEDIF(A2,B2,"M")

| C2 | | ⋮ | ✕ | ✓ | *fx* | =DATEDIF(A2,B2,"M") |

◢	A	B	C	D	E
1	**Start Date**	**End Date**	**Months**		
2	12/06/2015	12/01/2017	23		
3					

DAYS Function

The DAYS function returns the number of days between two dates.

Syntax

DAYS (end_date, start_date)

Arguments

Argument	Description
start_date	Required. This argument represents the start date of the period.
end_date	Required. This argument represents the end date of the period.

Example

In this example, we want to calculate the number of days between two dates, December 1, 2018, and December 1, 2019.

Formula:

=DAYS(B2, A2)

C2		▼ :	✕ ✓	f_x	=DAYS(B2, A2)	

◢	A	B	C	D	E	F
1	**Start Date**	**End Date**	**Days**			
2	12/1/2018	12/1/2019	365			
3						
4						

If you're entering the dates directly into the formula bar, you need to enclose them in quotation marks.

For example:

DAYS ("12/01/18", "12/01/2019") will return 365 days.

9.5 Find Data with VLOOKUP

The VLOOKUP function (vertical lookup) is the most commonly used lookup function in Excel. This is the updated version of the legacy LOOKUP function. The old LOOKUP function is still available in Excel for backward compatibility, but it is no longer recommended. Use VLOOKUP going forward as it is more robust and better supported in the latest versions of Excel.

VLOOKUP enables you to find one piece of information in a workbook based on another piece of information. For example, if you have a *Products* table, you can find and return the *Product Code* by providing the *Product Name* to the VLOOKUP function.

Syntax

VLOOKUP (lookup_value, table_array, col_index_num, [range_lookup])

Arguments

Argument	Description
Lookup_value	Required. What value are you searching for? This is the lookup value. Excel will look for a match for this value in the leftmost column of your chosen range. You can provide a value here or a cell reference.
Table_array	Required. What columns do you want to search? This is the lookup table containing the columns you want to include in your search e.g. A2:D10.
Col_index_num	Required. Which column contains the search result? Count from the first column to determine what this number should be, starting from 1.
Range_lookup	Optional. If you want an exact match, enter FALSE or 0 here. However, if an approximate match is OK then enter TRUE or 1. For TRUE, you would need to sort the leftmost column in ascending order for correct results. This is an optional argument and if left out it will default to TRUE.

Example

In the example below, we use VLOOKUP to find the *Price* and Reorder Level of a product by entering the *Product Name* in cell G2. The formula is in cell G3 and as you can see from the image below, it searches the table for *Dried Pears* and returns the price from the next column.

Formula Explanation

To look up the **Price** for Dried Pears the formula is:

=VLOOKUP(G2, B2:D46, 2, FALSE)

The function uses a lookup_value from cell **G2** to search a table_array which is **B2:D46**.

The col_index_num is **2** so it returns a value from the second column in the table_array, which is the **Price** column.

The range_lookup is **FALSE** meaning we want an exact match.

To look up the **Reorder Level** for Dried Pears we use the same formula and just change the column that contains the search result (**col_index_num**) to 3 so that it returns a value from the third row of the table array.

=VLOOKUP(G2, B2:D46, **3**, FALSE)

In this case, the VLOOKUP search for Dried Pears returns a Reorder Level of **10**.

9.6 Manipulate Text

If you work with Excel extensively, there are going to be occasions when you would need to use functions to manipulate text, especially when you work with data imported from other programs. For example, you may want to strip off part of a text value or rearrange text.

Tip: The **Flash Fill** command on the Home tab now enables you to carry out many text manipulation tasks for which you would previously use functions. See chapter 2 for how to use Flash Fill to manipulate text values.

LEN Function

The LEN function returns the number of characters in a text string. The LEN function is useful when used with other Excel functions like MID where you can use LEN to return a value for one of its arguments.

Syntax

LEN(text)

Argument	Description
Text	Required. This is a text string or a cell reference containing the text for which you want to find the length. Spaces are counted as characters.

Example

In the following example, we use the LEN function to count the number of characters in an item code. The example also demonstrates how the LEN function can be used in combination with the MID function to return part of a string.

	B2	▾	:	×	✓	fx	=LEN(A2)	

◢	A	B	C	D
1	Text	Formula	Formula text	Description
2	NWTCFV-88	9	=LEN(A2)	Length of item code
3	NWTCFV-90	90	=MID(A3,8,LEN(A3)-7)	MID (used with LEN) extracts only the numbers in the item code
4	NWTCFV-91	NWTCFV	=MID(A4,1,LEN(A4)-3)	MID (used with LEN) extracts only the letters in the item code
5				
6				
7				
8				
9				

=LEN(A2)

This simply returns the length of text value in its argument.

=MID(A3,8,LEN(A3)-7)

MID is used here with LEN to extract only the numbers in the item code. The role of LEN is to return the length of the whole string so we can use it in our formula to extract the part that we want.

=MID(A4,1,LEN(A4)-3)

MID is used here with LEN to extract only the letters in the item code

MID Function

The MID function enables you to extract a portion of a text string based on a starting position you specify and the number of characters you want to extract.

Syntax

MID(text, start_num, num_chars)

Arguments

Argument	Description
Text	Required. A text string or a cell reference containing the characters you want to extract.

| Start_num | Required. This is a number representing the starting position of the first character you want to extract in *text*. The first character in *text* starts with 1, the second is 2 and so on. |
| Num_chars | Required. This is a number that specifies the number of characters you want to extract from *text*. |

Notes:

- If the start_num argument is larger than the length of the string in our text argument, MID will return an empty text ("").

- MID will return the #VALUE! error if start_num is less than 1.

- MID returns the #VALUE! error if num_chars is a negative value.

Example

In the examples below, we use the MID function to extract characters from several text values.

B1			fx	=MID(A1,4,3)	
	A	B	C		D
1	01-345-4000	345	=MID(A1,4,3)	Extract the 3 characters in the middle of the serial number	
2	01-378-7890	378	=MID(A2,4,3)		
3	01-375-7891	375	=MID(A3,4,3)		
4	01-376-7892	376	=MID(A4,4,3)		
5					
6					
7	NWTCFV-88	88	=MID(A7,8,2)	Extract only the number portion of the item code	
8	NWTCFV-89	89	=MID(A8,8,2)		
9	NWTCFV-90	90	=MID(A9,8,2)		
10	NWTCFV-91	91	=MID(A10,8,2)		
11					
12					

Formula description

=MID(A1,4,3)

For this formula, A1 is the cell reference containing the string we want to extract text from - "01-345-4000". The first character we want to extract is 3 which starts at position 4, so we have 4 as our *start_num*. We want to return 3 characters in total, so we have 3 as the *num_chars*.

=MID(A7,8,2)

This formula has A3 as the text argument and 8 as the *start_num* as this is the first character we want to return from the string which has 10 characters. The *num_chars* argument is 2 as this is the number of characters we want to return.

The benefit of using formulas like these is that you create them once and use the fill handle of the first cell to copy the formula to the other cells.

9.7 Accessing More Functions in Excel

To access the full function library in Excel, click on the **Formulas** tab on the ribbon. You will see a list of command buttons for several categories of functions.

The functions are grouped under the following categories:
- Recently Used
- Financial
- Logical
- Text
- Date & Time
- Lookup & Reference
- Math & Trig
- Statistical
- Engineering
- Cube
- Information
- Compatibility
- Web

You can explore the various functions by clicking on the drop-down button for each one of the command buttons and you'll get a pop-up list of the functions related to each button.

Many of these functions are for specialist tasks and professions, so don't let them overwhelm you as you'll never get to use most of them. For example, the **Financial** functions are mostly going to be used by accountants, the **Engineering** functions are mostly used by engineers, etc.

The functions you've used the most will be listed under the **Recently Used** list for easy access.

To get more details about each function, mouseover a function name on the list and a small pop-up message will appear, giving you more details of the function and what arguments it takes. For example, if you mouseover the **IF** function, you will see the function description and the arguments it takes.

Getting More Help with Functions

To get more information on the use of any function in Excel, press **F1** to display the Help panel. Then type "Excel functions" in the search bar. This will give you a list of all the functions in Excel by category. You can locate the one you want and click on it to see more details on how it is used.

10. WORKING WITH TABLES

You can turn your Excel data into a table. When you create a table in Excel it is easier for you to manage and analyse your data. You also get built-in sorting, filtering, Banded Rows, and the ability to add a Total Row.

Before you create a table ensure there are no empty columns or rows in the data.

In the next example, we will convert the following range of data into a table.

	A	B	C	D	E
1	Last Name	First Name	Company	Job Title	Address
2	Bedecs	Anna	Company A	Owner	123 1st Street
3	Gratacos Solsona	Antonio	Company B	Owner	123 2nd Street
4	Axen	Thomas	Company C	Purchasing Represen	123 3rd Street
5	Lee	Christina	Company D	Purchasing Manager	123 4th Street
6	O'Donnell	Martin	Company E	Owner	123 5th Street
7	Pérez-Olaeta	Francisco	Company F	Purchasing Manager	123 6th Street
8	Xie	Ming-Yang	Company G	Owner	123 7th Street
9	Andersen	Elizabeth	Company H	Purchasing Represen	123 8th Street
10	Mortensen	Sven	Company I	Purchasing Manager	123 9th Street
11	Wacker	Roland	Company J	Purchasing Manager	123 10th Street
12	Krschne	Peter	Company K	Purchasing Manager	123 11th Stree
13	Edwards	John	Company L	Purchasing Manager	123 12th Stree
14	Ludick	Andre	Company M	Purchasing Represen	456 13th Street
15	Grilo	Carlos	Company N	Purchasing Represen	456 14th Street
16	Kupkova	Helena	Company O	Purchasing Manager	456 15th Stre

First, check that there are no empty columns or rows in your data:

1. Select any cell within the data and press **CTRL + A**.

2. Then press **CTRL + "."** a few times to move around the data.

Note: CTRL + A selects the data range in question. **CTRL + "."** moves around the four edges of the data so you can see where the data starts and ends.

10.1 Create an Excel Table

To create a table from your data:

1. Click on any cell within the data.

2. Click on the **Insert** tab and click on **Table** (in the **Tables** group).

3. A dialogue box will be displayed showing you the range to be used for the table. You can adjust the range here if necessary.

4. Click on the **My table has headers** checkbox to ensure that the first row of your table is used as the header.

Tip: If your table has no column headers, create a new row on top and add column headers. This makes it easier to work with tables in Excel.

5. Click **OK**.

The table will be created with your first row used as column headers.

	A	B	C	D	E
1	**Last Name**	**First Name**	**Company**	**Job Title**	**Address**
2	Bedecs	Anna	Company A	Owner	123 1st Street
3	Gratacos Solsona	Antonio	Company B	Owner	123 2nd Street
4	Axen	Thomas	Company C	Purchasing Represen	123 3rd Street
5	Lee	Christina	Company D	Purchasing Manager	123 4th Street
6	O'Donnell	Martin	Company E	Owner	123 5th Street
7	Pérez-Olaeta	Francisco	Company F	Purchasing Manager	123 6th Street
8	Xie	Ming-Yang	Company G	Owner	123 7th Street
9	Andersen	Elizabeth	Company H	Purchasing Represen	123 8th Street
10	Mortensen	Sven	Company I	Purchasing Manager	123 9th Street
11	Wacker	Roland	Company J	Purchasing Manager	123 10th Street
12	Krschne	Peter	Company K	Purchasing Manager	123 11th Street
13	Edwards	John	Company L	Purchasing Manager	123 12th Street
14	Ludick	Andre	Company M	Purchasing Represen	456 13th Street
15	Grilo	Carlos	Company N	Purchasing Represen	456 14th Street
16	Kupkova	Helena	Company O	Purchasing Manager	456 15th Street

Another way to quickly format a range as a table is to select the cells in the range and on the ribbon, select **Home > Format as Table.**

10.2 Choosing a Table Style

When you convert a range to a table, you will notice that a style with alternating row colours has been applied to the table. You can change this style if you want by selecting a new style from many options provided by Excel.

When you select any cell in the table, you'll see a **Design** tab on the ribbon. On this tab, you'll find the groups **Table Styles** and **Table Style Options.** Table Styles provides a number of predefined styles you can apply to your table while Table Style Options provides further options to format your table.

E	F	G	H	I	J
▾ Address	▾ City	▾ State/P ▾	Country/R ▾		
e 123 8th Street	Portland	OR	USA		
e 456 18th Street	Boston	MA	USA		
e 123 3rd Street	Los Angelas	CA	USA		
456 17th Street	Seattle	WA	USA		
123 1st Street	Seattle	WA	USA		
123 12th Street	Las Vegas	NV	USA		
789 19th Street	Los Angelas	CA	USA		

How to Apply a Table Style

1. Select a cell within the table.

2. On the **Design** tab, locate the **Table Styles** group and click on the drop-down button for the styles. A drop-down menu will show you more styles.

3. Mouseover each style to see a preview of how it would look on your worksheet.

4. When you find a style, click on it to apply it to your table.

Configure Table Style Options

Here you have several options for configuring the style of your table.

For example, you can change your table from **Banded Row** to **Banded Columns**. Banded rows are the alternating colours applied to your table rows.

Banded Rows is the default but if you want banded columns instead, uncheck **Banded Rows** and check **Banded Columns** to have your columns alternate in colour instead of your rows.

Note that if a new column or row is added to the table, it will automatically inherit the current table style. When you add a new row, any formulas applied to your table will also be copied to the new row.

10.3 Sorting Data in a Table

Before you begin sorting data, ensure there are no blank rows and blank columns.

Tip: To check for blank rows or columns, select a cell within the data and press **CTRL + A**. Then press **CTRL + "."** a few times. This moves the cursor around the four corners of the range so you can see the whole area.

Before you start sorting, also make sure your table header is a single row. If it is made up of more than one row, change it to a single row because it will make things a lot easier.

Sort by One Column

To quickly sort by one column in your table:

1.   Select a cell in the column you want to use for the sorting, for example, *Last Name*.

2.   On the **Data** tab, in the **Sort & Filter** group, click **AZ** (to sort the table in ascending order) or **ZA** (to sort the table in descending order).

Sort by Multiple Columns

A **Custom Sort** is required to sort a table by multiple columns.

Carry out the following steps to apply a custom sort:

1.   Select any cell within the data.

2.   On the ribbon, navigate to **Home** > **Sort & Filter** (in the Editing group).

3.   Select **Custom Sort…** from the drop-down menu. The sort dialogue box will be displayed.

Tip: Another way to launch the Custom Sort screen is to click on **Data** > **Sort** (in the Sort & Filter group).

4. Click on **Add Level**.

5. Under **Column**, select the column you want to **Sort by** from the drop-down list. Select the second column you want to include in the sort in the **Then by** field. For example, Sort by Last Name and First Name.

6. Under **Sort On**, select **Values**.

7. Under **Order**, select the order you want to sort on i.e. **A to Z** for ascending order, and **Z to A** for descending order.

8. Click **OK** when done.

You can add additional columns to your sort. Starting with Excel 2016 you can have up to 64 sort levels. For each additional column that you want to sort by, repeat steps 4-7 above.

10.4 Filtering Table Data

Excel provides an array of options to filter your data so that you can view data that meets a certain criterion. Filters provide a quick way to work with a subset of data in a range or table. When you apply the filter you temporarily hide some of the data so that you can focus on the data you need to view.

How to filter data:

1. Select a cell within the data that you want to filter.

2. Click on **Home** > **Sort & Filter** > **Filter** (or click **Data** > **Filter**).

3. You will get filter arrows at the top of each column.

4. Click the drop-down arrow of the column you want to filter. For example, Price.

5. Uncheck **Select All** and check the values you want to use for the filter.

6. Click **OK**.

	A	B	C	D	E
1	Product Code	Product Name	Price	Reorder Level	Category
16	NWTSO-41	Clam Chowder	$9.65	10	Soups
17	NWTB-43	Coffee	$46.00	25	Beverages
18	NWTCA-48	Chocolate	$12.75	25	Candy
19	NWTDFN-51	Dried Apples	$53.00	10	Dried Fruit & Nuts
20	NWTG-52	Long Grain Rice	$7.00	25	Grains
21	NWTP-56	Gnocchi	$38.00	30	Pasta
22	NWTP-57	Ravioli	$19.50	20	Pasta
23	NWTS-65	Hot Pepper Sauce	$21.05	10	Sauces
24	NWTS-66	Tomato Sauce	$17.00	20	Sauces
25	NWTD-72	Mozzarella	$34.80	10	Dairy Products
26	NWTDFN-74	Almonds	$10.00	5	Dried Fruit & Nuts
27	NWTCO-77	Mustard	$13.00	15	Condiments
28	NWTDFN-80	Dried Plums	$3.50	50	Dried Fruit & Nuts
29	NWTB-81	Green Tea	$2.99	100	Beverages
30	NWTC-82	Granola	$4.00	20	Cereal

The filter drop-down arrow changes to a funnel icon to show that the column is filtered. If you look at the row heading numbers, you'll see that they're now blue, indicating which rows are included in the filtered data.

To remove the filter, click on **Clear** in the **Sort & Filter** group. The filter will be removed, and all data will be displayed.

Applying a Custom Filter

Select the filter drop-down arrow and then select one from the following:

- **Text Filters** - this is available when the column has a text field or has a mixture of text and numbers: Equals, Does Not Equal, Begins With, Ends With, or Contains.

- **Number Filters** - this option is only available when the column contains only numbers: Equals, Does Not Equal, Greater Than, Less Than, or Between.

- **Date Filters** - this option is only available when the column contains only dates: Last Week, Next Month, This Month, and Last Month.

- **Clear Filter from 'Column name'** - this option is only available if a filter has already been applied to the column. Select this option to clear the filter.

When you select any of the first 3 options you will get a dialogue box – **Custom AutoFilter**.

Select **And** if both conditions must be true. Alternatively, select **Or** if only one of the conditions needs to be true.

Enter the values you want to use for the filter.

For example, to view rows with a number that is within a certain range, select **Number Filters > Between** and then enter the values in the two boxes provided.

For the example in the image above, we're filtering the *Price* column so that only rows between $2 and $10 are shown.

To change the order of the filtered results, click the filter drop-down button, and then select either **Sort Largest to Smallest** or **Sort Smallest to Largest**.

For a text sort column, it would be **Sort A to Z** or **Sort Z to A.**

10.5 Adding a Totals Row to Your Table

You can add totals to a table by selecting the **Total Row** check box on the **Design** tab. Once added to your worksheet, the Total Row drop-down button allows you to add a function from a list of options.

To add totals to your table:

1. Select a cell in a table.

2. Select **Design > Total Row**. A new row is added to the bottom of the table. This is called the **Total Row**.

3. On the total row drop-down list, you have a choice of functions to select from, like **Average, Count, Count Numbers, Max, Min, Sum, StdDev, Var,** and more.

NWTS-65	Hot Pepper Sauce	$21.05	10 Sauces
NWTS-66	Tomato Sauce	$17.00	20 Sauces
NWTS-8	Curry Sauce	$40.00	10 Sauces
NWTSO-41	Clam Chowder	$9.65	10 Soups
NWTSO-98	Vegetable Soup	$1.89	100 Soups
NWTSO-99	Chicken Soup	$1.95	100 Soups
Total		$713.06 ▾	
		None	
		Average	
		Count	
		Count Numbers	
		Max	
		Min	
		Sum	
		StdDev	
		Var	
		More Functions...	

Tip: If you need to add a new row of data to your table at some later point you need to uncheck **Total Row** on the **Design** tab, add the new row, and then recheck **Total Row**.

10.6 Removing Table Attributes

On some occasions, you may want to reverse a table back to a normal range.

Carry out the following steps to convert a table to a range:

1. Click anywhere inside the table so that the cell pointer is inside the table.

2. Click on the **Design** tab (this shows up when you click in the table).

3. In the Tools group on the Design tab, click on **Convert to Range**.

4. Click **Yes** at the prompt to confirm the action.

The table will now be converted to a normal range of cells without Excel's table attributes. Now, you may still have the banded-rows format that was applied as part of the table's format when it was converted. This formatting does not affect the behaviour of the range, but you can remove it if you want.

You can carry out the following steps to clear the formatting:

1. Select the range.

2. Click on the **Home** tab.

3. In the Editing group, click on **Clear** > **Clear Formats**.

11. INTRODUCTION TO PIVOT TABLES

A n Excel PivotTable is a powerful tool that enables you to dynamically calculate, summarise, and analyse data from different perspectives.

Note: A copy of the sample data used for the examples in this chapter is available in the downloadable file that comes with this book. See the introductory chapter for the download link for the file.

11.1 Preparing Your Data

Some preparation is required to get a set of data ready for a PivotTable. The source data used for a PivotTable needs to be organised as a list or converted to an Excel table (this is recommended although not a pre-requisite).

A few steps to prepare the source data for a PivotTable:

1. The data should have column headings in a single row on top.

2. Remove any temporary totals or summaries.

3. The data cannot have empty rows, so, delete any empty rows.

4. Ensure you do not have any extraneous data surrounding the list.

5. Ideally, you may want to create an Excel table with the data (although it is not a pre-requisite).

	A	B	C	D	E	F	G	H
1	Employee	Product	Customer	Order Date	Ship City	Item Cost	No. of Items	Total Cost
2	Anne Hellung-Larsen	Cora Fabric Chair	Acme LTD	11/24/2016	Las Vegas	$475.00	20	$9,500.00
3	Jan Kotas	Lukah Leather Chair	Elgin Homes	05/13/2016	New York	$345.00	9	$3,105.00
4	Mariya Sergienko	Habitat Oken Console Table	Mecury Builders	04/28/2016	Las Vegas	$36.00	28	$1,008.00
5	Michael Neipper	Hygena Fabric Chair	Infinity Homes	11/06/2016	Portland	$407.00	23	$9,361.00
6	Anne Hellung-Larsen	Harley Fabric Cuddle Chair	Elgin Homes	07/16/2016	New York	$803.00	20	$16,060.00
7	Jan Kotas	Windsor 2 Seater Cuddle Chair	B&B Seaside	04/27/2017	Denver	$302.00	8	$2,416.00
8	Mariya Sergienko	Fabric Chair	B&B Seaside	06/26/2016	Los Angelas	$425.00	11	$4,675.00
9	Laura Giussani	Verona 1 Shelf Telephone Table	Home Designers	04/07/2016	Milwaukee	$282.00	8	$2,256.00
10	Anne Hellung-Larsen	Floral Fabric Tub Chair	Acorn USA	08/17/2016	Memphis	$158.00	2	$316.00
11	Jan Kotas	Fabric Chair in a Box	Infinity Homes	04/20/2017	Portland	$857.00	28	$23,996.00
12	Mariya Sergienko	Slimline Console Table	Apex Homes	11/01/2016	Chicago	$534.00	29	$15,486.00
13	Nancy Freehafer	Collection Martha Fabric Wingback Chair	Empire Homes	09/24/2017	Boise	$137.00	15	$2,055.00
14	Nancy Freehafer	Slimline Console Table	Apex Homes	04/15/2017	Chicago	$433.00	16	$6,928.00
15	Nancy Freehafer	Fabric Wingback Chair	Express Builders	09/03/2016	Miami	$210.00	2	$420.00
16	Nancy Freehafer	Fabric Chair in a Box - Denim Blue	Impressive Homes	04/23/2016	Seattle	$634.00	14	$8,876.00
17	Nancy Freehafer	Tessa Fabric Chair	Acorn USA	02/10/2017	Memphis	$252.00	23	$5,796.00
18	Robert Zare	Collection Bradley Riser Recline Fabric Chair	Northern Contractors	01/05/2016	Salt Lake City	$281.00	5	$1,405.00
19	Michael Neipper	Fabric Wingback Chair	Home Designers	05/15/2017	Milwaukee	$405.00	30	$12,150.00
20	Mariya Sergienko	Tessa Fabric Chair	Infinity Homes	05/11/2017	Portland	$472.00	5	$2,360.00

Once the data has been prepared, we can now create a PivotTable.

11.2 Creating a Pivot Table

To create a PivotTable:

1. Click on any cell in your range or table.

2. On the Insert tab, click on the PivotTable button.

The **Create PivotTable** dialogue will be displayed.

Create PivotTable	? ✕
Choose the data that you want to analyze	
⦿ Select a table or range	
Table/Range: Sheet1!$A$1:$H$49	⬆
○ Use an external data source	
Choose Connection...	
Connection name:	
○ Use this workbook's Data Model	
Choose where you want the PivotTable report to be placed	
⦿ New Worksheet	
○ Existing Worksheet	
Location:	⬆
Choose whether you want to analyze multiple tables	
☐ Add this data to the Data Model	
	OK Cancel

Excel will figure out the table or range you intend to use for your PivotTable and it will select it in the **Table/Range** field. If this is not accurate then you can manually select the range by clicking on the up arrow on the field.

The next option on the screen is where you want to place the PivotTable. The default location is a new worksheet. It is best to have your PivotTable on its own worksheet, separate from your source data, so you want to leave the default selected here.

3. Click on **OK**.

A new worksheet will now be created with a PivotTable placeholder, and on the right side, you'll see a dialogue box - **PivotTable Fields**.

The PivotTable tool has four areas where you can place fields:

Rows, **Columns**, **Values**, and **Filters**.

To add a field to your PivotTable, select the checkbox next to the field name in the PivotTables Fields pane. When you select fields, they are added to their default areas. Non-numeric fields are added to the **Rows** box. Date and time fields are added to the **Columns** box. Numeric fields are added to the **Values** box.

You can also drag fields from the list to one of the four areas you want to place it. To move one field to another, you can drag it there.

To remove a field from a box, click on it and click **Remove Field** from the pop-up menu. You can also just uncheck it in the fields list or drag it away from the box and drop it back on the fields list.

Example

In this example, let's say we want a summary of our data that shows the total spent by each Customer.

1. Select the **Customer** field on the list and it will be added to the Rows box. The PivotTable will also be updated with the list of customers as row headings.

2. Next, select the **Total Cost** field and this will be added to the **Values** box.

The PivotTable will now be updated with the **Sum of Total Cost** for each Customer.

3	Row Labels ▼	Sum of Total Cost
4	Acme LTD	13226
5	Acorn USA	13292
6	Apex Homes	33082
7	B&B Seaside	48997
8	Elgin Homes	54504
9	Empire Homes	9355
10	Express Builders	11004
11	Home Designers	52322
12	Impressive Homes	14775
13	Infinity Homes	85612
14	Mecury Builders	17760
15	Northern Contractors	2001
16	Orion Spaces	4806
17	Grand Total	360736

So, as you can see, we have been able to get a quick summary of our data with just a few clicks. If we had hundreds of thousands of records, this could have taken many hours to accomplish if done manually.

We can add more values to the table by dragging them to the Values box from the list.

For example, if we wanted to add the total number of items per customer, we'll select **No. of Items** on the list or drag it to the **Values** box.

Drag fields between areas below:

▼ Filters ||| Columns

                   Σ Values   ▼

≡ Rows   Σ Values

Customer   ▼   Sum of Total Cost   ▼

                      Sum of No. of Items   ▼

☐ Defer Layout Update   Update

This will add the **Sum of No. of Items** for each customer to the PivotTable as shown in the image below.

Row Labels ▼	Sum of No. of Items	Sum of Total Cost
Acme LTD	43	13226
Acorn USA	53	13292
Apex Homes	73	33082
B&B Seaside	88	48997
Elgin Homes	123	54504
Empire Homes	40	9355
Express Builders	14	11004
Home Designers	94	52322
Impressive Homes	31	14775
Infinity Homes	143	85612
Mecury Builders	52	17760
Northern Contractors	7	2001
Orion Spaces	33	4806
Grand Total	**794**	**360736**

To view the summary from the perspective of **Products**, i.e. the total number of items sold and the total cost for each product, we would put **Product** in the Rows box and both **Total Cost** and **No. of Items** in the Values box.

To view the summary from the perspective of **Employees**, we would place **Employee** in the Rows box, and **No. of Items** and **Total Cost** in the Values box.

Here we see the data summarised by Employee i.e. how many items each employee sold, and the revenue generated.

Row Labels ▾	Sum of No. of Items	Sum of Total Cost
Andrew Cencini	40	21418
Anne Hellung-Larsen	149	53969
Jan Kotas	110	70865
Laura Giussani	26	18690
Mariya Sergienko	176	78334
Michael Neipper	105	40203
Nancy Freehafer	181	75256
Robert Zare	7	2001
Grand Total	**794**	**360736**

If we want to see the number of items sold per city, we would place **Ship City** in the Rows box and **No. of Items** in the Values box.

	Row Labels ▾	Sum of No. of Items
3		
4	Boise	40
5	Chicago	106
6	Denver	45
7	Las Vegas	95
8	Los Angelas	43
9	Memphis	53
10	Miami	44
11	Milwaukee	94
12	New York	93
13	Portland	143
14	Salt Lake City	7
15	Seattle	31
16	**Grand Total**	**794**

Summarising Data by Date

To display the columns split into years, drag a date field into the Columns box, for example, Order Date. The PivotTable tool will automatically generate PivotTable fields for Quarters and Years. Once these fields have been generated, you should remove the Order Date field from the Columns box and place in the Quarter or Year field, depending on which one you want to use for your summary.

To display the row headings by date, place **Order Date** (or your date field) in the Rows box.

This will produce the following results.

Sum of Total Cost	Column Labels		
Row Labels	2016	2017	Grand Total
Jan	39569	7772	47341
Feb		22819	22819
Mar	5502	1854	7356
Apr	22724	57618	80342
May	3105	14510	17615
Jun	24021	596	24617
Jul	16060		16060
Aug	316	12141	12457
Sep	42763	9615	52378
Oct	16752		16752
Nov	34347	9756	44103
Dec	18896		18896
Grand Total	224055	136681	360736

Applying Formatting

As you can see, we can dynamically change how we want to view our data with just a few clicks. When you're happy with your summary, you can then apply formatting to the appropriate columns. For example, you could format **Sum of Total Cost** as **Currency** before any formal presentation of the data.

The good thing about PivotTables is that you can explore different types of summaries with the pivot table without changing the source data. If you make a mistake that you can't figure out how to undo, you can simply delete the PivotTable worksheet and recreate the PivotTable in a new worksheet.

11.3 Filter and Sort a PivotTable

On some occasions, you may want to limit what is displayed in the PivotTable. You can sort and filter a PivotTable just like you can do to a range of data or an Excel table.

To filter a PivotTable:

1. Click on the AutoFilter (down arrow) on the Row Labels cell.

The pop-up menu provides a list of the row headings in your PivotTable. You can select/deselect items on this list to limit the data being displayed in the PivotTable.

2. Uncheck **Select All.**

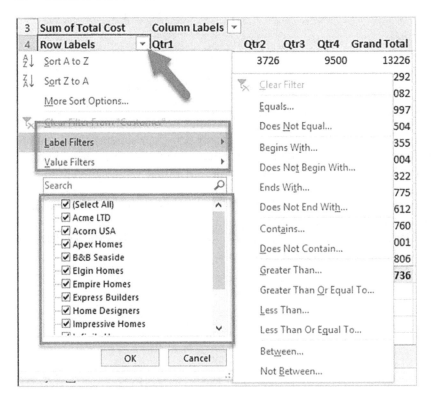

3. Scroll through the list and manually select the items you want to display.

4. Click **OK**.

The PivotTable will now show only the selected columns.

Applying a Custom Filter

You can also use the **Label Filters** and **Value Filters** menu commands to apply a custom filter to your PivotTable. This is done in the same way as you would do for a range or table. Please see the chapter titled **Sort and Filter Data** in this book for detailed steps on how to apply a custom filter.

Sorting PivotTable Data

To arrange the order of your data in a PivotTable you use the same sorting methods you would use for a range or table.

- Click on the **AutoFilter** button on the column named **Row Labels**.

- Click on **Sort A to Z** (to sort in ascending order) or **Sort Z to A** (to sort in descending order). If your column headings are dates, then you'll get **Sort Oldest to Newest** (for ascending) and **Sort Newest to Oldest** (for descending).

12. CREATING CHARTS

Excel charts provide a way to present your data visually. As the saying goes, *a picture is worth a thousand words*. Some of us don't absorb numbers as easily as others because we're more visual and this is where charts come in. A visual representation may sometimes create more of an impact with your audience.

In this chapter, we will cover how to create charts quickly with the Quick Analysis tool, how to create charts from the Insert tab, how to edit and format chart labels, and how to apply different styles to your charts.

Preparing Your Data

To prepare your data for charting, you'll need to organise it in a list with only the items you want to report on. Leave out any extraneous data and grand totals you don't want on the chart. Ideally, you should have column headings. The example below has *Product Name* and *Total Sales* as column headings.

	A	B
1	**Product Name**	**Total Sales**
2	Chai	$1,800.00
3	Beer	$3,400.00
4	Coffee	$4,600.00
5	Green Tea	$200.00
6	Tea	$1,400.00
7	Chocolate Biscuits Mix	$900.20
8	Scones	$1,000.00
9	Brownie Mix	$1,200.49
10	Cake Mix	$1,500.99
11	Granola	$400.00
12	Hot Cereal	$500.00
13	Chocolate	$1,200.75
14	Fruit Cocktail	$3,900.00
15	Pears	$100.30
16	Peaches	$1,000.50

12.1 Creating a Chart via the Quick Analysis Tool

The Quick Analysis tool appears as a button on the bottom-right of your selection when you select a range of data in Excel. The Quick Analysis button offers a host of features for quickly adding conditional formatting, totals, tables, charts, and Sparklines to your worksheet.

To generate a chart using the quick analysis tool:

1. Select the data range you want to use for your chart. The Quick Analysis button is displayed at the bottom-right of the selection.

2. Click on the Quick Analysis button and then click on **Charts**. You'll get a list of recommended charts.

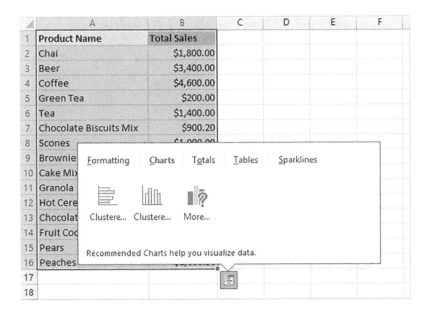

3. Click on the second option to generate a column chart.

	A	B	C	D	E	F	G	H	I	J	K
1	Product Name	Total Sales									
2	Chai	$1,800.00									
3	Beer	$3,400.00									
4	Coffee	$4,600.00									
5	Green Tea	$200.00									
6	Tea	$1,400.00									
7	Chocolate Biscuits Mix	$900.20									
8	Scones	$1,000.00									
9	Brownie Mix	$1,200.49									
10	Cake Mix	$1,500.99									
11	Granola	$400.00									
12	Hot Cereal	$500.00									
13	Chocolate	$1,200.75									
14	Fruit Cocktail	$3,900.00									
15	Pears	$100.30									
16	Peaches	$1,000.50									

A floating chart will be created in the same worksheet as your data. You can click and drag this chart to another part of the screen if necessary.

To create another type of chart, like a pie chart, for example, you can click on the **More...** option on the Quick Analysis menu to show a list of all chart types.

Tip: Another way to create a quick chart is to select the data and press the **F11** key to generate a chart of the default type on a new chart sheet. The default chart created would be the column chart, unless you've changed the default chart. To create an embedded chart using this method (i.e. in the same worksheet as the data) press the **Alt + F1** keys together.

12.2 Creating a Chart via the Excel Ribbon

The **Charts** group in the Insert tab has several commands to create different types of charts. You can click on a chart type, for example, the pie chart icon, to display a list of charts options available for that chart type.

Alternatively, you can launch the **Insert Chart** dialogue box that shows a list of all the chart types you can create in Excel.

To create a chart from the Insert Chart dialogue:

1. Select the range of data for your chart.

2. On the ribbon, click on Insert > Recommended Charts > All Charts.

    The **Insert Chart** dialogue is displayed.

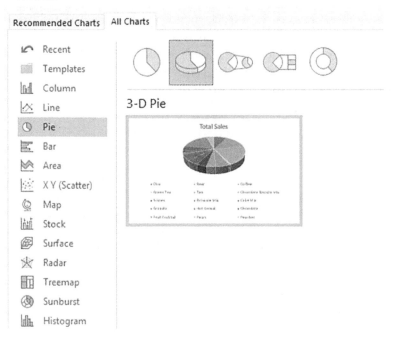

3. Select the type of chart you want to create from the list of charts on the left.

4.   Click **OK**.

A floating chart will be created in the same worksheet as your data. You can click and drag this chart to another part of the screen if necessary.

To delete a chart, simply select the chart and press the **Delete** key.

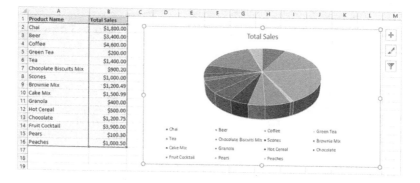

After creating the chart you'll get a new tab on the ribbon called **Design**. This tab provides many options to edit and style your chart. We will be covering editing the chart axis labels and style later in this chapter.

12.3 Customising Charts

After creating a chart, you have several tools available for formatting and customising the chart to your liking. For example, you can swap the axis, change/adjust the data source, update the chart title, adjust the layout, apply a chart style, and apply a theme colour to your chart.

To demonstrate some of these options, let's say we need to create a chart with four quarters of sales.

	A	B	C	D	E
1	Sales by Quarter				
2	Product	QTR1	QTR2	QTR3	QTR4
3	Chai	300	300	200	400
4	Beer	300	200	400	300
5	Coffee	350	400	500	500
6	Green Tea	250	150	100	300
7	Tea	100	400	100	500
8	Chocolate Biscu	320	200	100	300
9	Scones	250	500	200	100
10	Brownie Mix	350	400	550	200
11	Cake Mix	200	370	300	200
12	Granola	250	100	200	400
13	Hot Cereal	350	500	300	200
14	Chocolate	350	200	500	500
15	Fruit Cocktail	200	230	250	200
16	Pears	100	200	300	450
17	Peaches	200	300	200	600
18					

To create the chart:

1. Select the range with the data, including the column headers and row headers.

2. Click on **Insert > Recommended Charts.** You're presented with the **Insert Chart** dialogue box with several chart recommendations for your data.

3. Select the **Clustered Column** option.

4. Click **OK.**

A chart will be created and added to your worksheet.

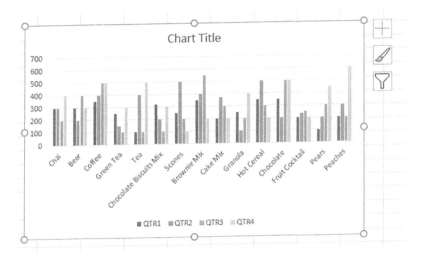

Switching the X and Y Axes

You can switch the values Excel applies to the vertical axis (also called the y-axis) and horizontal axis (also called the x-axis).

To switch the values applied to the axes:

1. Select the chart.

2. Click **Design > Switch Row/Column.**

This will swap the values applied to the vertical and horizontal axes.

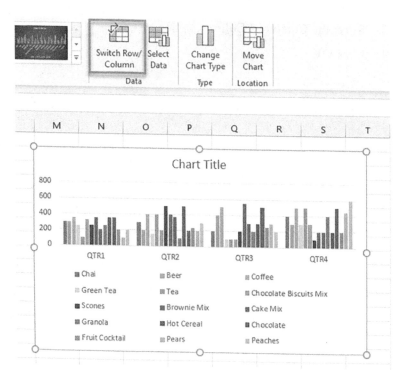

To swap the values back, simply click the **Switch Row/Column** button again.

Change the Data Source

To change the data used as the source of the chart, do the following:

1. Click the **Select Data** button on the **Design** tab. The **Select Data Source** dialogue box will be displayed.

2. Select the up arrow that is on the **Chart data range** field. This will change it to a down-pointing arrow.

3. Select the cells you want in the worksheet area and click on the down-pointing arrow to return to the **Select Data Source** screen.

4. Click **OK** to confirm the change.

The new data source will now be used for the chart.

Adding Axis Titles

When you create a new chart, you'll see "Chart Title" as a placeholder that needs to be edited with the title of the chart. There are also no labels at the axis, and we may want to add them to the chart.

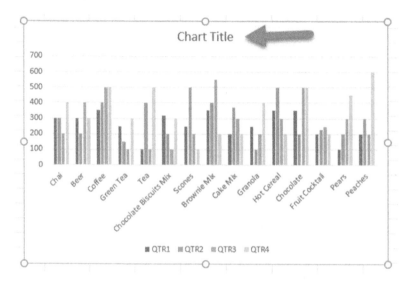

To change the **Chart Title,** you can simply click on it and type in the title. Alternatively, you can select the name from a field on your worksheet. For example, if we wanted our chart title to be *Sales by quarter,* which is in cell **A1** of our worksheet, we would click on the Chart Title label and in the formula bar, enter "**=A1**". This will use the value in cell A1 for our chart title.

We can also add titles down the left-hand side and at the bottom of the chart. These are called axis titles. The left side is the *y*-axis while the bottom is the *x*-axis.

To change the layout of your chart, click on **Design > Quick Layout**.

You'll get a pop-up with several chart layouts. With the chart selected, you can mouseover each layout to view more details about it and get a preview of how your chart will look with that layout. A few of the options provide axis titles as well as moving the legend to the right of the chart. If you want a layout with both axis titles, then **Layout 9** would be a good pick.

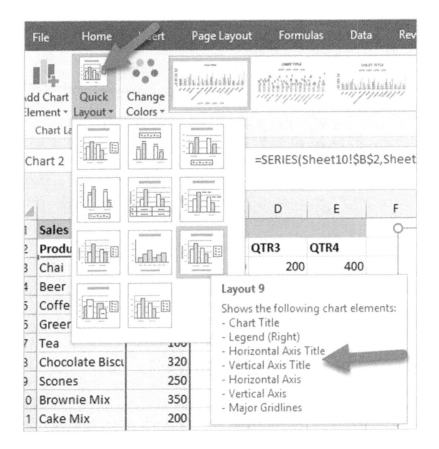

If we select **Layout 9**, we get a chart with labels that we can edit to add titles to the x-axis and y-axis.

You can edit the axis labels as described above. You can click on the labels and type in the text directly or pull the text from your worksheet area by typing in a cell reference, for example, **=A1**, assuming cell A1 as the text you want for that label.

Chart Styles

When you click on the chart, the **Design** tab shows up on the ribbon. On this tab, you have an array of **Chart Styles** you can choose from to change the look and colour of your chart.

To change the colour of the plot area:

1. Click on the plot area to select it (this is the centre of the chart) and it will be selected.

2. With the plot area selected, click on the **Format** tab on the ribbon.

3. Click the drop-down button in the **Shape Styles** group.

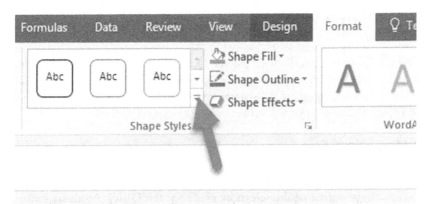

4. You'll get a pop-up with many **Theme Styles** to choose from for the format of the plot area. You can mouseover each one to see a preview of how your chart would look like if selected.

5. When you find the one you like, click on it to select it.

12.4 Creating Sparkline Charts

In the following example, we'll use the Quick Analysis tool to add sparklines to our worksheet. Sparklines are mini-charts you can place in single cells to show the visual trend of your data. Excel 2019 allows you to quickly add Sparkline charts to your worksheet in a few steps.

Adding a Sparkline:

1. Select the data you want to create a Sparkline chart for. At the lower-right corner of the selection, you'll see the **Quick Analysis** tool.

2. Click on the Quick Analysis tool to open a pop-up menu of Quick Analysis options - **Formatting, Charts, Totals, Tables,** and **Sparklines.**

3. Click on Sparklines and then select one option from **Line, Column,** or **Win/Loss.**

For this example, the **Line** option was selected. The sparklines will be created in the cells immediately to the right of the selected values.

⊿	A	B	C	D	E	F	G	H	I	J	K	L	M	N
1	Expenses													
2		Jan	Feb	Mar	Apr	May	Jun	Jul	Aug	Sep	Oct	Nov	Dec	
3	Building 1	$45.00	$22.40	$33.70	$44.90	$21.90	$22.00	$10.00	$23.00	$23.00	$23.00	$23.00	$23.00	
4	Building 2	$31.00	$33.00	$32.00	$41.00	$31.00	$42.00	$11.00	$55.00	$55.00	$67.00	$33.00	$44.00	
5	Building 3	$34.00	$60.00	$21.00	$30.00	$55.00	$60.00	$23.00	$45.00	$56.00	$21.00	$25.00	$76.00	
6														

Formatting a Sparkline Chart

To format your Sparkline chart, click on it to select it.

On the ribbon, click on the **Design** tab. In the **Style** group, you'll see various options to edit and style your sparkline chart.

Use the following options to design your sparkline:

- Click on **Line**, **Column**, or **Win/Loss** to change the chart type.

- You can check **Markers** to highlight specific values in the Sparkline chart.

- You can select a different **Style** for the Sparkline.

- You can change the **Sparkline Color** and the **Marker Color**.

- Click on **Sparkline Color** > **Weight** to change the width of the Sparkline.

- Click on **Marker Color** to change the colour of the markers.

- Click on **Axis** to show the axis, if the data has positive and negative values.

13. PRINTING YOUR WORKSHEET

The world is increasingly becoming paperless, however, on some occasions, you may need to print out a hardcopy of your worksheet. You may want to print it as part of a report or to present it to others. Excel provides a rich array of features that allow you to print your data in many ways.

Page Setup

Before you print your document, you may need to change some settings to get the page layout the way you want it. The Page Setup screen enables you to configure several page layout settings in one area.

To launch the Page Setup screen, click on the **Page Layout** tab, and in the **Page Setup** group, click on the dialog box launcher.

The Page Setup screen will be displayed.

There are several settings on this page that you can configure to get the layout exactly how you want it for your printed document.

Orientation

On the **Page** tab, set the orientation to **Landscape**. This is best for printing worksheets unless you have specific reasons to use portrait.

Scaling

Under scaling you have two options:

1. **Adjust to:** This option enables you to scale the font size of your document up or down. 100% means it will print in normal size. For example, if the normal size of your content is larger than one page but you would like it to print as one page, you would reduce the percentage to less than 100%.

2. **Fit to:** This option enables you to choose how wide and how tall you want your document. So, for example, you may choose to fit the width to one page and have more than one page for the length.

Paper Size

The default paper size is A4. However, if you are printing to another paper size you can change it here.

Margins

On the Margins tab, you can change the size of the Top, Bottom, Left, and Right margins, including the size of the Header and Footer.

Header/Footer

You can insert a header or footer, e.g. a page number, in your document using this tab. You can either select an option from the drop-down list or enter a custom header/footer by clicking on **Custom Header** or **Custom Footer**.

When you're done, click **OK** to save your changes and close the Page Setup window.

Setting the Print Area

You need to set the Print Area so that unpopulated parts of the worksheet are not included in your print as this could result in blank pages. You can set the print area in the Page Setup screen however, it is easier to use the **Print Area** command button on the Excel ribbon.

To set the print area:

1. Select the area in the worksheet that contains the data you want to print.
2. On the **Page Layout** tab, click on the **Print Area** button.

3. Select **Set Print Area**.

Note: If you wish to clear the print area at any point, click on the Print Area button and select **Clear Print Area**.

Preview and Print Your Worksheet

Click on **File** to display the Backstage view, then click **Print** from the menu on the left.

This will display the Print screen. There are several settings you can adjust here to change the page layout, many of which are also available in the Page Setup screen.

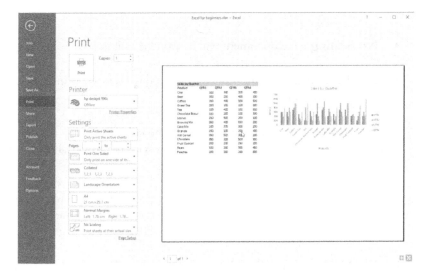

The options on this screen are pretty much self-explanatory and very similar for most Office applications. However, we'll touch on the ones you'll most likely need to set.

Printer

This option allows you to choose the printer you want to print to. If your printer is online (i.e. it has been configured in Windows and is turned on) then it will be available for selection here. You also have the option of printing to an electronic document like PDF, OneNote, Microsoft XPS Document Writer etc.

Settings

Print Active Sheets is the default. Leave this option selected if you want to print only the active worksheet. If your workbook has more than one worksheet and you want to print the entire workbook, then click on the drop-down list and select **Print Entire Workbook** from the list. If you have selected a range and you want to print only those cells, then use the **Print Selection** option.

The last option on this page is **scaling**. If you have not set the scale in the Page Setup screen there are four predefined scaling options to choose from here.

- **No Scaling** - the document will be printed as it is with no scaling.

- **Fit Sheet on One Page** – all columns and rows in the print area will be scaled into one page.

- **Fit All Columns on One Page** – all the columns in the print area will be scaled down to fit one page, however, the rows can carry on into other pages.

  Tip: I find this option to be the most appropriate if you have many rows of data. Always try to scale the columns into one page, if possible, so that you can see a full row of data on one page.

- **Fit All Rows into One Page** – all rows in the print area will be scaled to fit one page, however, the columns can carry on into other pages.

Previewing Your Document

The right side of the screen provides a preview of how your printed document would look. If you have more than one page, use the navigation buttons at the bottom of the screen to view the other pages.

Note: Always preview your document before printing it to ensure you're happy with the layout. This will save you a ton of ink and paper!

The other settings on the Print page are self-explanatory.

When you're happy with your settings and the preview, click on the **Print** button to print your document.

14. SECURING YOUR WORKBOOK

E xcel enables you to protect your workbook with a password to prevent others from editing your data, deleting worksheets, or renaming worksheets in the workbook.

Important! Before you protect your workbook with a password, ensure that you've got the password written down and stored in a safe place where it can be retrieved if necessary. Without an advanced password cracking tool, it is impossible to gain access to an Excel file that has been password-protected if the password has been forgotten.

How to set a password for your Excel workbook

To set a password on your Excel workbook:

1. Click **File** > **Info** > **Protect Document** > **Encrypt with Password**.

2. At the prompt enter your password, then confirm it.

3. Click on **OK** after confirming the password.

4. Save and close the workbook.

5. When you reopen the workbook, it will prompt you for the password.

Removing a Password from an Excel File

On some occasions, you may want to remove a password from an Excel file. The process of setting a password encrypts the file so you'll need to remove the encryption. Carry out the following steps to remove the password.

1. Open the workbook and enter the password in the Password box.

2. Click **File** > **Info** > **Protect Workbook** > **Encrypt with Password**.

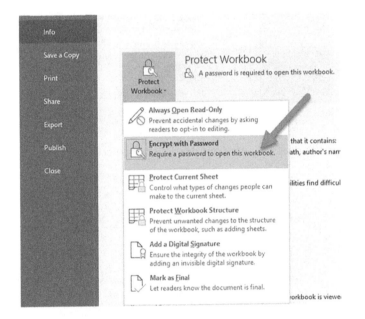

This will display the **Encrypt Document** dialogue box.

3. Delete the contents of the Password box.

4. Click OK.

Save the file and close it. When you open the file again it will not challenge you for a password.

AFTERWORD: NEXT STEPS

Thank you for buying and reading this book. I hope it has been helpful to you. The topics have been kept at the beginner to intermediate level to ensure readers who are new to Excel are not overwhelmed. However, if you have any comments or suggestions for how this book can be improved even further, please feel free to contact me at:

nathangeorgeauthor@gmail.com

More Help with Excel

For more help with Excel, you can visit Excel's official online help site.

https://support.office.com/en-gb/excel

This is a comprehensive help centre for Excel. Although not an organised tutorial like this book, it is useful when you're looking for help on a specific topic. You'll also find resources like Excel templates that you can download and use as the starting basis for your worksheets.

APPENDIX: KEYBOARD SHORTCUTS (EXCEL FOR WINDOWS)

The Excel Ribbon comes with new shortcuts called Key Tips. To see Key Tips, press the **Alt** key when Excel is the active window.

The following table lists the most frequently used shortcuts in Excel 2019.

Keystroke	Action
F1	Opens Excel's Help window
Ctrl+O	Open a workbook
Ctrl+W	Close a workbook
Ctrl+C	Copy
Ctrl+V	Paste
Ctrl+X	Cut
Ctrl+Z	Undo
Ctrl+B	Bold
Ctrl+S	Save a workbook
Ctrl+F1	Displays or hides the ribbon
Delete key	Remove cell contents

Alt+H	Go to the Home tab
Alt+H, H	Choose a fill color
Alt+N	Go to Insert tab
Alt+A	Go to Data tab
Alt+P	Go to Page Layout tab
Alt+H, A, then C	Center align cell contents
Alt+W	Go to View tab
Shift+F10, or Context key	Open context menu
Alt+H, B	Add borders
Alt+H,D, then C	Delete column
Alt+M	Go to Formula tab
Ctrl+9	Hide the selected rows
Ctrl+0	Hide the selected columns

Access Keys for Ribbon Tabs

To go directly to a tab on the Excel Ribbon, press one of the following access keys.

Action	Keystroke
Open the Tell me box on the Ribbon.	Alt+Q
Open the File page i.e. the Backstage view.	Alt+F
Open the Home tab.	Alt+H
Open the Insert tab.	Alt+N
Open the Page Layout tab.	Alt+P
Open the Formulas tab.	Alt+M
Open the Data.	Alt+A
Open the Review.	Alt+R
Open the View.	Alt+W

To get a more comprehensive list of Excel for Windows Shortcut, press **F1** to open Excel Help and type in "Keyboard shortcuts" in the search bar.

GLOSSARY

Absolute reference
This is a cell reference that doesn't change when you copy a formula containing the reference to another cell. For example, $A$3 means the row and column have been set to absolute.

Active cell
The cell that is currently selected and open for editing.

Alignment
The way a cell's contents are arranged within that cell. This could be left, centred or right.

Argument
The input values a function requires to carry out a calculation.

AutoCalculate
This is an Excel feature that automatically calculates and displays the summary of a selected range of figures on the status bar.

AutoComplete
This is an Excel feature that completes data entry for a range of cells based on values in other cells in the same column or row.

Backstage view
This is the screen you see when you click the File tab on the ribbon. It has a series of menu options to do with managing your workbook and configuring global settings in Excel.

Cell reference
The letter and number combination that represents the intersection of a column and row. For example, B10 means column B, row 10.

Conditional format
This is a format that applies only when certain criteria are met by the cell content.

Conditional formula
A conditional formula calculates a value from one of two expressions based on whether a third expression evaluates to true or false.

Dialog box launcher
In the lower-right corner of some groups on the Excel ribbon, you'll see a diagonal down-pointing arrow. When you click on the arrow it launches a dialogue box containing several additional options for that group.

Excel table
This is a cell range that has been defined as a table in Excel. Excel adds certain attributes to the range to make it easier to manipulate the data as a table.

Fill handle
This is a small square on the lower-right of the cell pointer. You can drag this handle to AutoFill values for other cells.

FillSeries
This is the Excel functionality that allows you to create a series of values based on a starting value and any rules or intervals included.

Formula
An expression used to calculate a value.

Formula bar
This is the area just above the worksheet grid that displays the value of the active cell. This is where you enter a formula in Excel.

Function
A function is a predefined formula in Excel that just requires input values (arguments) to calculate and return a value.

Named range
A group of cells in your worksheet given one name that can then be used as a reference.

OneDrive
This is a cloud storage service provided by Microsoft which automatically syncs your files to a remote drive, hence providing instant backups.

PivotTable
This is an Excel summary table that allows you to dynamically summarise data from different perspectives. PivotTables are highly flexible, and you can quickly adjust them, depending on how you need to display your results.

Quick Access Toolbar
This is a customisable toolbar with a set of commands independent of the tab and ribbon commands currently on display.

Relative reference
Excel cell references are relative references by default. This means, when copied across multiple cells, they change based on the relative position of columns and rows.

Ribbon
This is the top part of the Excel screen that contains the tabs and commands.

Sort
A sort means to reorder the data in a worksheet in ascending or descending order by one or more columns.

Sparkline
This is a small chart that visually represents data in a single worksheet cell.

Validation rule
This is a test that data must pass to be a valid entry in a cell.

Workbook
This is the Excel document itself and it can contain one or more worksheets.

Worksheet
A worksheet is like a page in an Excel workbook.

x-axis
The horizontal axis of a chart where you could have time intervals etc.

y-axis
This is the vertical axis of a chart, which usually depicts value data.

INDEX

Absolute Cell Reference, 103
Autofill, 32
AutoFilter, 58
AutoSave, 23
AutoSum, 90
AVERAGE function, 129
AVERAGEIF, 141
AVERAGEIFS, 141
Cells
   Alignment, 67
   Merge & Center, 66
Charts
   column chart, 188
   Pie-chart, 190
Conditional formatting, 76
COUNT function, 132
COUNTIF, 141
COUNTIFS, 142
Custom AutoFilter, 60
Custom Filter, 58
Custom Number Formats, 71
Custom Sort, 54
DATE function, 144
DATEDIF function, 149
DAYS function, 151
Dialog Box Launcher, 21
Excel Table

Banded Columns, 166
Banded Rows, 166
Fill Handle, 32
Find and Replace, 51
Flash Fill, 36
Format Painter, 74
Freeze panes, 43
IF function, 135
   Advanced IF functions, 140
   Nested IF Functions, 139
LEN function, 155
MAX function, 131
MEDIAN function, 131
Merge & Center, 66
MID function, 156
MIN function, 131
Mixed Cell Reference, 106
Named Range, 114
Number Formats, 69
Office Themes, 12
Password, 208
PivotTable, 174
Quick Access Toolbar, 21
Quick Analysis tool, 188
Quick Sort, 53
Quick Sum, 96
Relative Cell Reference, 103

Resizing cells, 62
Ribbon, 20
Sparklines, 200
SUM function, 126
SUMIF, 142

TIME function, 100
Total Row. *See* Excel Table
VLOOKUP function, 153
Worksheet
 Applying themes, 45

ABOUT THE AUTHOR

Nathan George is a computer science graduate with several years' experience in the IT services industry in different roles which included Excel VBA programming, Excel training, and providing end-user support to Excel power users. One of his main interests is using computers to automate tasks and increase productivity. As an author, he has written several technical and non-technical books.

OTHER BOOKS BY AUTHOR

Excel 2019 Advanced Topics

Leverage More Powerful Tools to Enhance Your Productivity

Whether you have basic Excel skills or you're a power user, *Excel 2019 Advanced Topics* is full of methods and tips that will enable you to take advantage of more powerful tools in Excel to boost your productivity. *Excel 2019 Advanced Topics* covers a selection of advanced topics relevant to productivity tasks you're more likely to perform at home or at work. This book does not only show you how to use specific features, but also in what context those features need to be used.

Excel 2019 Advanced Topics explains how to automate Excel with macros, use What-If Analysis tools to create alternate data scenarios and projections, analyze data with pivot tables and pivot charts, debug formulas, solve complex data scenarios with advanced functions, use data tools to consolidate data, remove duplicate values from lists, create financial formulas to carry out financial calculations, and much more.

Available at:

US: https://www.amazon.com/dp/1080491252

UK: https://www.amazon.co.uk/dp/1080491252

Excel 2019 Functions

70 Top Excel Functions Made Easy

Do you want to delve more into Excel functions and leverage their full power in your formulas? Excel functions are predefined formulas that make it easier and faster to create solutions for your data. *Excel 2019 Functions* provides a detailed coverage of 70 of the most relevant Excel functions in various categories including logical, reference, statistical, financial, math, and text functions.

Learn how to use many advanced functions introduced in Excel 2016/2019 like the IFS function which can replace convoluted nested IF functions. This book also comes with lots of Excel examples which you can download as Excel files, so you can copy and use the formulas in your own worksheets. *Excel 2019 Functions* will be a great resource for you whether you're a beginner or experienced with Excel.

Available at:

US: https://www.amazon.com/dp/1796379948

UK: https://www.amazon.co.uk/dp/1796379948

67247914R00126

Made in the USA
Middletown, DE
10 September 2019